W9-BSS-851

3 1965 0017 5569

SEP **2 8** 2009

DATE DUE

South Carolina

SOUTH CAROLINA BY ROAD

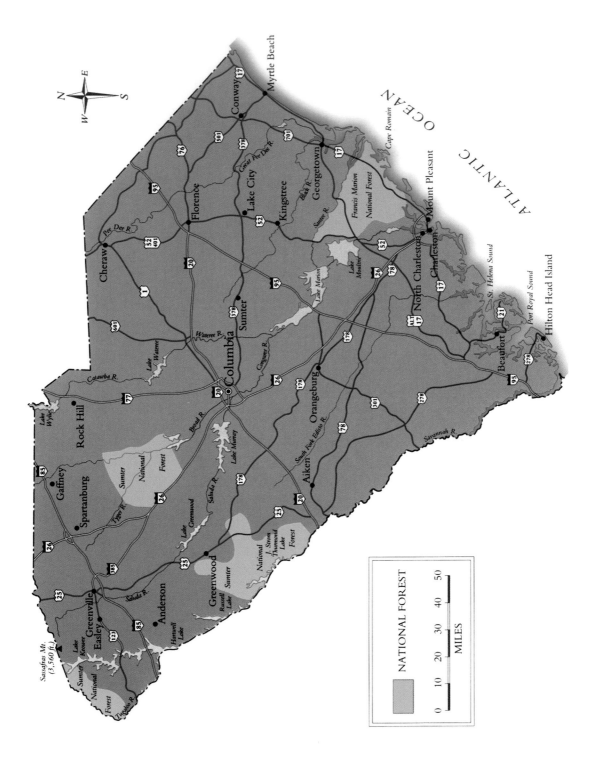

South Carolina

Nancy Hoffman and Joyce Hart

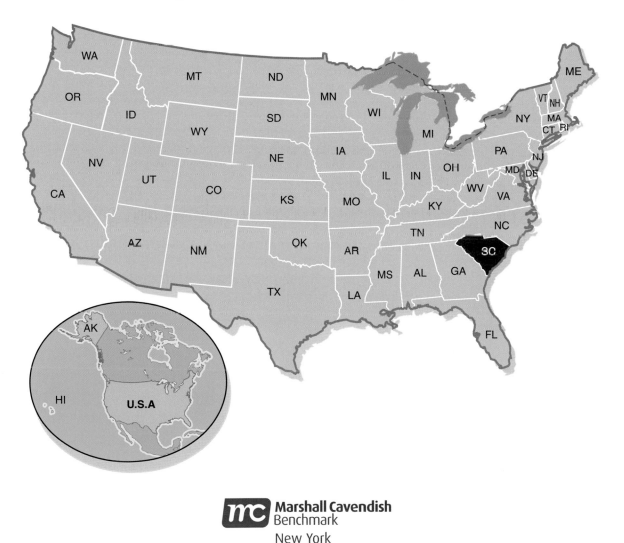

mc **Marshall Cavendish**
Benchmark
New York

Marshall Cavendish Benchmark
99 White Plains Road
Tarrytown, NY 10591-5502
www.marshallcavendish.us

Library of Congress Cataloging-in-Publication Data
Hoffman, Nancy, 1955–
South Carolina / by Nancy Hoffman and Joyce Hart.—2nd ed.
p. cm. — (Celebrate the states)
Summary: "Provides comprehensive information on the geography, history, wildlife, governmental
structure, economy, cultural diversity, peoples, religion, and landmarks of South Carolina"—Provided
by publisher.
Includes bibliographical references and index.
ISBN 978-0-7614-4034-5
1. South Carolina—Juvenile literature. I. Hart, Joyce, 1954– II. Title.

F269.3.H64 2010
975.7—dc22
2008038266

Editor: Christine Florie
Co-Editor: Denise Pangia
Publisher: Michelle Bisson
Art Director: Anahid Hamparian
Series Designer: Adam Mietlowski

Photo research and layout by Marshall Cavendish International (Asia) Private Limited—
Thomas Khoo, Benson Tan and Shawn Wee

Cover photo by Photolibrary

The photographs in this book are used by permission and through the courtesy of, *Photolibrary*:
back cover, 10, 12, 14, 17, 20, 21, 22, 23, 24, 26, 37, 41, 45, 52, 56, 58, 65, 70, 72, 80,
99, 102, 104, 107, 111, 115, 116, 119, 132; *Corbis*: 8, 16, 32, 79, 88, 90, 98, 110, 126; *Getty
Images*: 13, 29, 40, 43, 50, 55, 61, 76, 83, 85, 89, 96, 101, 120, 121, 122, 125, 127, 129, 130;
Photolibrary / Alamy: 19, 28, 31, 33, 38, 95, 105, 131, 133, 134, 135, 136; *Naional Geographic
Society Image Collection*: 51; *Lonely Planet Images*: 64, 117; *AP Photo / Mary Ann Chastain*: 74.

Printed in Malaysia
1 3 5 6 4 2

Contents

South Carolina Is . . .

South Carolina is scenic . . .

"It is a very beautiful place. . . . The flowers very fragrant. Orange trees, some kind of Palms, tamarinds, Magnolias, and other tropical plants. Gay birds and butterflies helped to make the pretty scene. Mocking birds abounded."

—Union soldier John W. M. Appleton

. . . and it is varied.

"When you have a great variety of habitats, then nature will fill these spaces with a great variety of animals and plants."

—South Carolinian naturalist Rudy Mancke

South Carolinians are hospitable.

"Come in, kind friend and browse around our yard; Perhaps by looking Carefully, you'll catch a glimpse of God."

—South Carolinian poet Clarke Willcox

They are passionate about preserving their heritage.

"Our historical buildings and beautiful natural areas—these have been left to us to care for, appreciate and cherish."

—South Carolina WNSC-TV host Mary Long

"I know I can't save a whole culture, but as an artist I can help create greater awareness."

—Gullah artist Jonathan Green

"The sweet smell of the South, of camellias and azaleas, cling to Beaufort's ancient and historic buildings."

> —from the book *Around America*, TV news analyst and author Walter Cronkite

South Carolina leaves its mark . . .

"I was born and raised on a Carolina sea island and I carried the sunshine of the low-country, inked in dark gold, on my back and shoulders."

> —South Carolinian author Pat Conroy

. . . and inspires dedicated service for its people.

"The people in this administration are dedicated to the idea that we don't serve ourselves: we're employed by, and we serve, the people of South Carolina."

> —Mark Sanford, governor of South Carolina

South Carolina has both a diverse history and a varied landscape, which inspire the people who live there and attract those who do not. As the eighth state to join the Union, South Carolina has a history that extends to the very roots of American culture. Some of the major historical events that took place in South Carolina proved to be pivotal in charting the course for the United States. Reminders of the state's early history draw visitors who are interested in the architecture and life of the colonial and antebellum eras. In addition to the historical landmarks, South Carolina has a wide range of landforms to explore. From the Blue Ridge Mountains in the northwestern corner of the state, where snow sometimes falls, to the Grand Strand of sun-baked, sandy beaches along the Atlantic Ocean, South Carolina is a place in which residents as well as tourists from all around the world can enjoy the treasures of nature.

Chapter One

A Southern Jewel

Located in the southeastern corner of the United States, South Carolina has boundaries that make the state resemble a jagged triangle. On the state's eastern border is the Atlantic Ocean, with wide, sandy beaches covering much of the northern shoreline, and swamps and marshlands framing the southern coast. The state's southwestern border is formed by the Savannah River, which separates South Carolina from Georgia. The northern border is the state's longest, where it meets North Carolina.

Measuring 273 miles (439 kilometers) across at the widest point from east to west, and 219 miles (352 km) from north to south, the state is relatively small. It covers only 32,020 square miles (82,931 square km) and ranks fortieth in size among the fifty states. Despite its small size, however, South Carolina has abundant geographic variety.

The terrain of South Carolina slopes gradually downward from the state's northwestern corner to the Atlantic Coast in the east. South Carolina shares three distinct natural regions with other states that run along the East Coast. Like North Carolina and Virginia, the state's far western side contains the Blue Ridge Mountains. In the middle

At the edge of the Blue Ridge Mountains lies Table Rock State Park, one of South Carolina's most popular parks since it was built in the 1930s.

of the state is the Piedmont Plateau. The Coastal Plain runs along the eastern portion of the state. The two highest regions, the Blue Ridge Mountains and the Piedmont, make up the area South Carolinians refer to as the upcountry. In contrast, Carolinians call the Coastal Plain the lowcountry.

HOW THE PALMETTO STATE GOT ITS NICKNAME

The nickname Palmetto State may have been coined in the nineteenth century. Here is one story about how South Carolina got its nickname. During the American Revolution Colonel William Moultrie oversaw the construction of a fort on Sullivan's Island. The fort, which was located at the entrance to the Charles Town Harbor, was made of sand and palmetto trees (as shown on the right). These palmetto trees grew profusely along the coast. On June 28, 1776, Moultrie and his troops repelled a British sea attack on this fort, partly because the British cannonballs sank into the fort's soft walls without doing much damage. The South Carolinian troops went on to win the battle. Later, in honor of this victory, the palmetto tree was placed on the state flag, was named the state tree, and appeared on the state seal.

LAND AND WATER

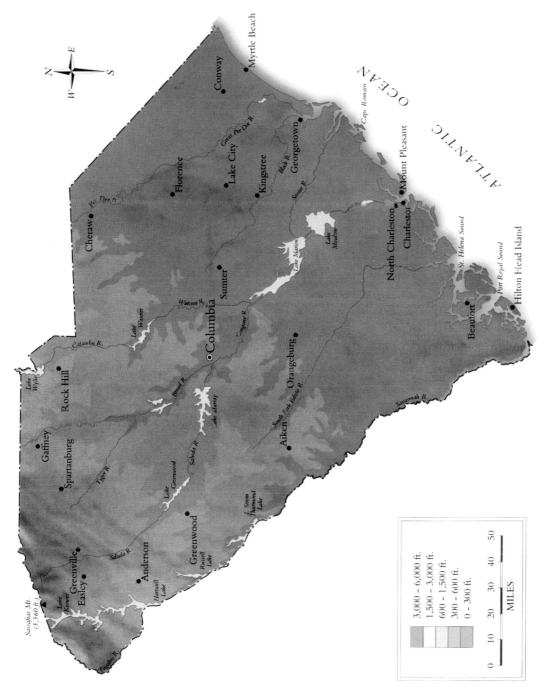

Myrtle Beach

Conway

ATLANTIC OCEAN

Cape Romain

Great Pee Dee R.

Florence

Lake City

Kingstree

Black R.

Georgetown

Santee R.

Cheraw

Pee Dee R.

Mount Pleasant

Lake Marion

Lake Moultrie

North Charleston

Charleston

St. Helena Sound

Sumter

Wateree R.

Port Royal Sound

Hilton Head Island

Lake Wateree

Congaree R.

Columbia

Catawba R.

Beaufort

Orangeburg

South Fork Edisto R.

Lake Wylie

Rock Hill

Broad R.

Lake Murray

Savannah R.

Aiken

Gaffney

Spartanburg

Saluda R.

Tiger R.

Lake Greenwood

Strom Thurmond Lake

Greenwood

Saluda R.

Russell Lake

Greenville

Anderson

Easley

Hartwell Lake

Sassafras Mt.
(3,560 ft.)

Lake Keowee

Tugaloo R.

3,000 – 6,000 ft.
1,500 – 3,000 ft.
600 – 1,500 ft.
300 – 600 ft.
0 – 300 ft.

MILES

0   10   20   30   40   50

THE UPCOUNTRY

The Blue Ridge Mountain region in the northwestern corner rises above rolling hills and valleys. The state's highest point in the mountain region is Sassafras Mountain, which stands 3,560 feet (1,085 meters) above sea level.

Not far away from Sassafras Mountain is an escarpment in the Blue Ridge Mountains. The escarpment—a steep slope in the earth that separates the mountains from the Piedmont—extends from Virginia to Georgia. In South Carolina this escarpment forms the Jocassee

Lake Jocassee, with its crystal clear water, is located in a pristine mountain environment.

Gorges, a series of steep-sided rock chasms through which mountain rivers flow on their way to the Piedmont. The escarpment also creates many spectacular waterfalls. This mountainous area of western South Carolina sometimes receives more than 75 inches (191 centimeters) of precipitation per year. The rain collects in the area's many rivers and creeks, such as the Toxaway, Whitewater, Horsepasture, Bearcamp, and Eastatoe. The rivers, in turn, feed Lake Jocassee, a man-made lake that covers 7,500 acres (3,035 hectares) and is 300 feet (91 m) deep. The lake was formed by the construction of a 1,750-foot-long (533-m-long) hydroelectric dam. In describing the Jocassee Gorges area, Greg Lucas of the South Carolina Department of Natural Resources once said, "This is as wild as it gets as far as South Carolina goes."

THE CAROLINA PARAKEET

The Eastatoe River was named for an ancient American Indian tribe. The name translates to "green bird," a reference that most likely was connected with the Carolina parakeet. This small green bird, the only parrot native to eastern North America, was last seen in the Eastatoe Valley. By 1904 the bird was extinct.

The Piedmont Plateau makes up the second part of the upcountry. In South Carolina the plateau stretches 11,000 square miles (17,700 sq km) between the Blue Ridge Mountains and the Coastal Plain and covers most of the northwestern portion of the state. South Carolina's Piedmont area ranges from 400 to 1,400 feet (122 to 427 m) above sea level and consists of a wide belt of gentle hills. The land in the Piedmont slants toward the southeast, causing rivers to run swiftly across the landscape. Many years ago these surging waters were harnessed to generate hydroelectric power for the many factories that were built along the rivers' banks. Today the Piedmont remains home to most of the state's manufacturing. The Piedmont's rivers flow over what is referred to as a Fall Line. This marks the boundary between the Piedmont and the Atlantic Coastal Plain.

THE COASTAL PLAIN

Millions of years ago sharks and whales swam through a sea that covered the eastern half of South Carolina. The ocean coastline, in those ancient times, actually ran down what is now the middle of the state. Sand hills are all that is left of those ancient beaches. Today these hills are covered in pine forests.

Wetlands saturate the middle of the Coastal Plain. Rust-colored cypress trees and ancient oaks cast reflections in the shallow water. Webs of Spanish moss, a flowering plant with aerial roots, often hang from the trees. Water

Spanish moss grows on trees and absorbs nutrients from the air and rainfall.

hyacinth grows rapidly here, providing shelter and food for many kinds of animals.

As the crow flies, South Carolina's coastline runs 187 miles (301 km). But if you count the shoreline of all the bays, peninsulas, and islands, South Carolina has a little more than 2,800 miles (4,056 km) of flat, sandy beachfront property. Important bays along the coast include Little River Inlet, Winyah Bay, Charleston Harbor, and Port Royal Sound. Much of the northern portion of the state's coastline, from the North Carolina border to Winyah Bay, is called the Grand Strand, a continuous stretch of sand and beach communities.

Over a period of thousands of years the coast has eroded, and rivers have carried silt out to sea. Those remnants of land and small deposits of silt formed islands that extend from the Carolinas all the way down to the northern Florida coast. South Carolina's most prominent islands include Isle of Palms, Sullivan's Island, Kiawah Island, Edisto Island, Hilton Head Island, and Parris Island.

RIVERS AND LAKES

Waters from South Carolina's northwestern corner pour down the mountains, then rapidly move across the Piedmont Plateau and across the Coastal Plain. These waters are a great source of hydroelectric power and provide recreation opportunities for people and natural habitats for birds, mammals, and fish. Rivers and creeks join together and drain into the swamps and marshlands along the coast that border the Atlantic Ocean.

Important rivers in South Carolina include the Santee, which drains about 40 percent of the state's land, and the Pee Dee, which is the state's second-largest river. Along the border with Georgia is the state's third-

The Santee River, which is 143 miles (230 km) long, provides principal drainage and navigation for the central Coastal Plain of South Carolina.

largest river, the Savannah River, whose banks are often referred to as South Carolina's freshwater coast.

The Edisto River is the longest undammed blackwater river in the United States. The name "blackwater" refers to the river's color, which is very dark due to the acid that is released by the tree branches, roots, and leaves decaying in the slow-moving water. The Edisto River is 206 miles (332 km) long and ends at Edisto Beach, on the southeastern coast of the state on Edisto Island. Many other rivers in South Carolina are dammed, creating large man-made lakes, such as Lake Moultrie and Lake Marion, which are north of Charleston. The state has no naturally occurring large lakes.

THE WEATHER REPORT

Most of South Carolina lies in a humid, subtropical zone. This means that South Carolinians enjoy sultry summers and short, pleasant winters. In July temperatures reaching 90 degrees Fahrenheit (32 degrees Celsius) or above are common across the state, except in the Blue Ridge Mountains, where somewhat cooler temperatures prevail, and along the coast, where sea breezes provide relief from the heat. In winter the mountains protect the state from cold fronts coming down from the North. So January temperatures can average around 50 °F (10 °C) in the lowcountry but can drop to approximately 40 °F (4 °C) or lower in the upcountry.

South Carolina gets its fair share of rain. The mountains receive the most precipitation, averaging 70 to 80 inches (178 to 203 cm) each year. The coast comes close to matching this amount, receiving between 50 and 60 inches (127 and 152 cm) annually. The central area of the state receives the least, 40 to 50 inches (102 to 127 cm).

Violent storms can wreak havoc in South Carolina. One of the worst storms was Hurricane Hugo, which struck the South Carolina coast around Charleston in September of 1989. Hugo's 135-mile-per-hour (215-km-per-hour) winds devastated much of the lowcountry, leaving seventeen people dead, another 70,000 homeless, and 18,000 miles (28,968 km) of road impassable. The storm also uprooted one-third of the state's trees. Though South Carolina has been affected by other hurricanes in recent years, such as Floyd in 1999 and Charley in 2004, no storm since has been as strong or as destructive as Hurricane Hugo.

Homes along Folly Beach were severely damaged by Hurricane Hugo in 1989.

WEATHER-BREAKING RECORDS

On June 22, 2008, Charleston received 4.26 inches (108.2 cm) of rain in a twenty-four-hour period, breaking the city's all-time record. But this was not the greatest amount of precipitation to fall in a day in the state. That honor goes to Rimini, which received 24 inches (61 cm) of snow in February 1975. Twenty years prior to that, in 1954, South Carolinians could have used some of that wet stuff, as they were suffering the worst drought the state had ever seen.

All-time record high temperatures were recorded at Blackville and Calhoun Falls. The thermometers reached 111 °F (44 °C) in September of 1925 in both of those towns. Camden matched that same temperature on June 28, 1954. The coldest temperature Carolinians have ever felt occurred at Caesars Head on January 21, 1985, when temperatures fell to –19 °F (–28 °C).

FORESTS AND FLOWERS

Forests cover approximately two-thirds of South Carolina. Pines, tulip trees, and magnolias are found throughout the state. Hemlocks, cottonwoods, dogwoods, oaks, red maples, and hickories thrive in the mountains and on the Piedmont, while oaks, hickories, and cypresses grow in the swamplands, and palmetto trees and yucca plants grow near the coast. Much of the lowlands in South Carolina are known for the Spanish moss that drapes itself over the long limbs of live oaks.

CONGAREE NATIONAL PARK

On November 10, 2003, President George W. Bush designated a 22,000-acre (8,903-ha) tract of forest that runs along the Congaree River as the nation's fifty-seventh national park. Located only 20 miles (32 km) south of Columbia, the Congaree National Park, though one of the smallest national parks, is the largest tract of old-growth bottomland hardwood forest left in the United States. The term "old growth" means that a forest has been allowed to grow without human disturbance and therefore has an unspoiled ecosystem. In Congaree National Park visitors will find some of the largest and tallest trees in the eastern United States. Much of the land in this park has also been designated a National Wilderness Area, an International Biosphere Reserve, and a Globally Important Bird Area.

Perhaps the most spectacular time of year in South Carolina is spring, when it seems the whole state bursts into bloom. "Camellias strut their stuff, and, as if that were not enough, Azaleas follow soon to steal the show, to glorify corners where they grow," wrote South Carolinian poet Clarke A. Willcox.

The insect-eating Venus flytrap grows wild only in the Carolinas. Its sweet-tasting fluids attract insects. The plant's leaves act as traps, springing shut when the trigger hairs inside them are set off. When an insect flies too close, the leaves snap shut, and the plant digests its prey.

The Venus flytrap is a carnivorous plant that catches and digests animal prey such as insects and spiders.

ALL MANNER OF LIFE

Abundant white-tailed deer live in the Piedmont and Coastal Plains woods. Black bears, opossums, rabbits, raccoons, and alligators roam the swamps, which are also home to frogs, water moccasins, and copperhead snakes. This region also serves as a winter retreat for flocks of ducks and geese. Otters play in the rivers and streams, while bass, rockfish, and trout swim in the lakes. Clams, crabs, and shrimp live just off the Carolina coast. So do dolphins and giant turtles. Occasionally huge sperm whales and sharks can be spotted in South Carolina's coastal waters.

Carolina wrens, mockingbirds, catbirds, wild turkeys, and pelicans are only a few of the state's 360 species of birds. The anhinga, commonly

The white-tailed deer can be recognized by the characteristic white underside of its tail, which the deer shows when it's alarmed.

known as the snakebird, is plentiful in lowcountry swamps. It is called a snakebird because when partly submerged in water, its long neck and beak look and move just like a snake.

The anhinga, sometimes called a snakebird, is a dark-plumaged fish-eater that often swims with only its long neck above water. This resembles a snake ready to strike.

FISHEAGLES

When Francis Burn was a child, he used to go fishing with his grandfather. On one of those trips he watched a huge bird pick up a fish and fly away. He heard an elderly African-American man call the creature a fisheagle—the Gullah word for osprey. Burn never forgot that day. Many years later he started Fisheagle Tours, which takes people through the Santee Swamp, pointing out wildlife, including alligators, anhingas, and of course ospreys.

Adult ospreys are black on top and white underneath—the opposite of a bald eagle. They have white heads, except for a black crown and a broad black line from the bill through the eye to the back of the neck. No bird of prey is a better fisher than the osprey. They have unusually long legs, highly curved claws, and feet covered with small spikes to help them grip slippery prey.

Loggerhead sea turtles have been around for four million years. But unless an effort is made to save their habitat, they won't be around for much longer. Loggerheads, which can grow to the size of a large coffee table and weigh 400 pounds (181 kilograms), are found in warm, subtropical waters—like those off the coast of South Carolina. After twenty or more years of living in the sea, female turtles return to the beach where they were hatched to lay eggs.

The loggerhead sea turtle, named for its relatively large head, supports a powerful jaw that enables it to feed on hard-shelled prey.

Young turtles are in the greatest danger right after they hatch. Raccoons, crabs, and amberjacks (large fish) all prey on the hatchlings, but perhaps their deadliest enemy is human development. At night, away from artificial lights, water appears brighter than land. Scientists believe that this phenomenon guides loggerhead hatchlings to the water. But streetlights from beach resorts confuse the baby turtles. They crawl toward the lights and often get hit by cars or wander the beach until they are eaten or they dry up and die. Keeping beaches dark at night, trapping animals that eat hatchlings, and putting wire screens around nests can help the hatchlings survive. But much work still needs to be done to save this magnificent species.

In an effort to give these turtles better odds of survival, the South Carolina Aquarium in Charleston has begun a program called the Sea Turtle Rescue Program to rehabilitate sea turtles that have been injured or are sick. Some of the afflictions that the specialists at this facility encounter are bacterial and fungal infections, shock from cold temperatures, cuts from boat propellers, and bites from other animals. When a turtle regains its health, it is taken back to the beach and released. The first release of a recuperated turtle occurred in April 2003 on Edisto Island. Many more releases have happened since then. As South Carolinians become more aware of the fragile nature of the plants, animals, landscape, and bodies of water that surround them, they work harder to preserve the natural world that makes up this beautiful state.

Chapter Two

From Ancient to Modern Times

The history of the people who have lived on the land that is now South Carolina stretches to at least as far back as 11,000 B.C.E. Each historical era has left its mark on the land as well as on the people who have made their homes here. From the earliest people, who traveled across the mountains on foot, to the modern-day residents, who speed across the state on its many highways, the history of the land and the people of South Carolina is filled with fascinating tales of adventure, war, celebrations, and friendship.

THE ANCIENT PEOPLE

Though not much is known about the first inhabitants of what is now South Carolina, people have lived on this land for at least 11,000 years. In recent years some scientists have argued that people might have arrived even earlier, more than 30,000 years ago, but the evidence supporting

This monument, located in downtown Charleston, symbolizes the Confederate Defenders of Charleston that were stationed in Fort Sumter throughout the Civil War.

this theory has not yet been fully accepted. The most accepted theory is that the first inhabitants, the Clovis people, once lived in many regions of what is now the United States, including the area of present-day South Carolina.

During the last Ice Age, sea levels were low because so much ice was locked up in glaciers. The Clovis people crossed the Bering land bridge from Siberia and slowly migrated south and then across North America,

The Mississippians developed a complex culture based on a ritualistic relationship between the people and the land.

following game animals. Some of these people lived in nomadic groups throughout what is now South Carolina. One of the most abundant Clovis artifacts is a type of fluted stone spearhead called a Clovis point. This distinctive weapon has been found all across the United States.

Evidence of another ancient cultural group that came after the Clovis and is referred to as the Mississippian people has been found in many places in the United States. This group was known for the earthen mounds it built. Their earthen mounds were built to bury their dead and as places on which to perform rituals. In South Carolina the Congaree Swamp area, south of Columbia, contains such mounds. The Mississippian people lived here beginning around 900 C.E. Other ancient mounds in South Carolina include Auld Mound in Mount Pleasant, Hanckel Mound in Rockville, and Santee Indian Mound in Summerton.

MODERN-DAY AMERICAN INDIANS

By the time the first Europeans arrived in North America, there were at least twenty-nine distinct groups, or tribes, of American Indians living on the land that is now called South Carolina. It isn't clear whether these tribes are related to the ancient Clovis and Mississippian people, but the modern tribes had lived in this region for a long period of time.

One of the largest tribes, the Cherokee, lived mostly in the foothills of the mountains around today's Anderson, Greenville, and Spartanburg counties. The estimated Cherokee population in 1674 was about 50,000. They traded deerskins with the white settlers in exchange for tools and lived in large villages surrounded by tall fences. Another tribe that lived in the upcountry was the Catawba. Today the Catawba are the most prominent American Indian tribe remaining in the state. Their headquarters is located in Rock Hill.

The Yamasee people lived in the lowcountry, along the ocean shores of South Carolina. They lived off oysters and clams. The Pee Dee tribes lived along the riversides of the Pee Dee River, especially in Chesterfield and Marlboro counties. Today the Pee Dee are centered in McColl. The Pee Dee were farmers and fishermen. Other tribes include the Cusabo and Coosa, who lived along the coast, while the Edisto, Wateree, Santee, and Congaree settled in the

Everyday Cherokee attire consisted mainly of buckskin items lightly embellished with quills, beads, or shells, much like this.

marshes and the Piedmont. Many of the tribes were forced to move out of South Carolina by settlers who demanded the American Indians' land. Other tribes became completely extinct due to their inability to fight off some of the diseases, such as smallpox, the new settlers brought with them from Europe.

EUROPEANS ARRIVE

In 1521 a group of Spaniards set out from Santo Domingo, in the present-day Caribbean nation of the Dominican Republic, to explore the Carolina coast. They dropped anchor in Winyah Bay, near what is now Georgetown. A few days later the Spaniards lured some American Indians on board their ship and quickly set sail back to Santo Domingo. They presented seventy of their captives as slaves to Lucas Vásquez de Ayllón, the man who had sponsored the Spaniards' expedition. Ayllón, however, demanded that the American Indians be returned home.

Five years later Ayllón tried to establish a colony in what would become South Carolina. His party probably landed near the mouth of the Waccamaw River, where they established the first European settlement in the area. It was called San Miguel de Gualdape. The colonists soon faced a series of problems, including harsh weather and fighting among themselves and with the local Indian tribes. Many settlers, including Ayllón, died of disease. Before year's end the colony's survivors returned to Santo Domingo.

Early in the 1600s Great Britain claimed all of North America. In 1629 King Charles I of England gave a region called Carolana (later changed to Carolina), meaning "Land of Charles," to Sir Robert Heath. But Heath did nothing with the region. Later, King Charles II took the land back and gave it to eight men he called the Lords Proprietors. These men recruited people from the British-controlled Caribbean island of Barbados to help them settle the region.

In 1670 settlers established Charles Town as the first permanent European settlement in the region, at Albemarle Point. The Barbadians that the Lords Proprietors had

In the late 1600s English colonists grew cash crops, such as rice, which turned into a profitable export.

recruited experimented with growing several different crops. They were not very successful with some of them, such as sugar, tobacco, and cotton. But around 1680 they began growing rice, which many scholars believe was brought from Madagascar, an island off Africa. Rice thrived along the swampy Carolina coast and soon developed into a profitable export. Another money-making venture was the trading of animal furs and deerskins. There was a great demand for such goods in England, where deerskin clothing and furs had become very fashionable.

TRADE AND TENSION

The Cherokee and Catawba were the colonists' most important trading partners. At first the American Indians and settlers coexisted peacefully. But gradually more and more settlers moved into tribal territories, sometimes forcing the American Indians into slavery as they overtook their land.

In 1715 white settlers built a town on land belonging to the Yamasee. The American Indians attacked the settlers, killing four hundred people and starting a two-year war. Fifteen other tribes fought alongside the Yamasee. Eventually the colonists won the struggle, and the Yamasee fled south, to Florida.

The white settlers faced other challenges as well. Pirates threatened ships at the mouth of Charles Town Harbor. Finally, in 1718, dozens of pirates were captured and hanged, and South Carolina's troubles with high-seas treachery were over.

STEDE BONNET

Stede Bonnet, born sometime around 1688, was a pirate from the Caribbean island of Barbados. He was referred to as the "gentleman pirate," mostly because he was a somewhat successful landowner before he bought a sailing ship and re-created himself as a pirate. His main focus of criminal activity was up and down the Atlantic Coast of North America. After only one year of limited success

as a pirate, Bonnet was captured by a naval expedition determined to wipe out the pirates who had been destroying ships that attempted to come into the Charles Town Harbor. Bonnet was arrested, along with more than twenty of his men. All were tried and hanged in Charles Town on December 10, 1718, virtually bringing a halt to piracy in South Carolina's waters.

COLONIAL TIMES

Having battled both American Indians and pirates with little help from their British government, the colonists asked King George I to end the Lords Proprietors' rule. In 1729 the king declared the Carolinas (land that would later be divided into North and South Carolina) to be royal colonies, ruled by him.

By the mid-1700s Charles Town was a city of rich merchants, vacationing plantation owners, and black slaves. Its grand homes were the most

While the earliest settlers primarily came from England, colonial Charles Town was also home to a mixture of ethnic groups.

lavish in all the American colonies. The city's rich cultural life included theater, music, sumptuous food, and lots of parties. After visiting from Massachusetts, Josiah Quincy wrote, "in grandeur, splendor of buildings, decorations . . . and indeed almost everything [Charles Town] far surpasses all I ever saw or ever expected to see in America."

Of course the slaves who made this lifestyle possible did not share in the city's splendor. Although many of the methods and much of the technology for planting and harvesting rice had been introduced by West African slaves, these slaves received no profits from their efforts. A few blacks were able to buy their freedom and became farmers or craftsmen, but the majority remained enslaved.

Compared to the lavish ways of the lowcountry elite, life in the upcountry was hard. There, German, Swiss, Welsh, and Scotch-Irish immigrants worked small farms in wild territory. They owned few slaves,

THE STONO REBELLION

Some believe it was the language of drums that sparked one of the most serious slave revolts in American history. On September 9, 1739, a slave named Cato, born in Angola, Africa, led an uprising at Stono, South Carolina. By beating drums, Cato managed to gather a group of twenty African-born men and women. Twenty miles (32 km) west of Charles Town, at the Stono River, the rebel band broke into a store and seized weapons and ammunition. The plan was to march south to Florida and freedom. As they marched, beating drums and calling out "Liberty!" others joined them, and eventually they became an army of nearly one hundred slaves. They fought their way down the road, setting homes and barns on fire as they went.

But after advancing only 12 miles (19 km), they stopped to celebrate their victory. The revelry was premature. The delay gave slave owners time to organize. A white militia surrounded Cato and his band, and after ten days of fighting, about forty African slaves and forty whites were killed. Eventually Cato and the other slaves were captured and executed.

Following the Stono Rebellion South Carolina passed a law forbidding blacks to make or have drums. Later, North Carolina and Virginia passed similar laws.

had few belongings, and lived in crude log cabins. After passing through the region, Minister Charles Woodmason described the typical upcountry diet of pork, corn bread, and clabber (curdled milk) as "what in England is given to the hogs and dogs."

The upcountry was not adequately represented in colonial government. Over time this inequality between the poor upcountry farmers and the wealthier and more politically powerful lowcountry residents grew into hostility and mistrust. This conflict would become evident as the fight for independence from Britain grew more intense.

FIGHT FOR INDEPENDENCE AND EVENTUAL STATEHOOD

In 1763 Britain ended a war with France. The war had drained Britain's economy. To raise money, Britain began taxing its colonies. In 1765 the British Parliament passed the Stamp Act, which taxed colonists every time they bought newspapers, legal documents, or even playing cards. This tax so angered the people of Charles Town that some of them vandalized the homes of British sympathizers. Under pressure, Britain repealed the Stamp Act but replaced it with taxes on other goods.

While the citizens of Charles Town grew more irate, many upcountry farmers remained loyal to Britain. The taxes hardly affected them, and British treaties helped the farmers keep peace with the Cherokee, who dominated the region.

In 1775 the Revolutionary War broke out. About 140 battles were fought in South Carolina before the war's end. Many of these battles did not even include British troops. On one side were the American Patriots, or Whigs. On the other side were the Tories, the colonists who remained loyal to Britain. These two groups of colonists fought one another so often, it seemed the colonists were at war with themselves.

In May 1780 British troops captured Charles Town. But American leaders such as Thomas "the Gamecock" Sumter and Francis "the Swamp Fox" Marion continued to harass the British, making raids and then disappearing back into the swamps where the British couldn't follow.

Even the previously pro-British upcountry farmers rallied to the Patriots' cause after a group of British soldiers killed surrendering Americans near Lancaster. On October 7, 1780, a band of Blue Ridge Mountain frontiersmen surrounded British major Patrick Ferguson's encampments on Kings Mountain. Ferguson and nearly four hundred of his men were killed. The Battle of Kings Mountain turned the tide in the Southern Continental forces' favor. The war eventually ended in 1783. In that same year the city of Charles Town was renamed "Charleston" because South Carolinians thought it sounded less British.

Four South Carolina delegates were sent to Philadelphia in 1787 to help frame the U.S. Constitution. The delegates were John Rutledge, a lawyer and judge; Charles Cotesworth Pinckney, a planter and lawyer; Charles Pinckney, who later served as a U.S. senator between 1798 and 1801; and Pierce Butler, a wealthy landowner. For four months the representatives at the convention debated the many issues involved in creating a long-lasting document that would be the basis of law in the new country. From May 25 until September 17 delegates from the colonies worked toward an agreement. Each colony then took its turn in ratifying the final document. When South Carolina's representatives signed their names to the new Constitution on May 23, 1788, the colony became the eighth state of the Union.

The Battle of Kings Mountain, fought on October 7, 1780, was considered the turning point in the South in America's war for independence.

THE GROWING SLAVERY SYSTEM

In 1792 the invention of the cotton gin—a machine that quickly removes seeds from the plant's fiber—increased cotton production and profit in South Carolina. Within a few years cotton became the state's top crop. As the number of cotton plantations grew, so did the need for slaves to work them. Running contrary to the white slave owners' success was the rising tension over the issue of slavery.

Threats to South Carolina's slavery system came from both inside and outside the state. In 1822 a free black man named Denmark Vesey planned a slave revolt in Charleston. Vesey and thirty-four of his followers were executed when the scheme was exposed. Meanwhile, the number of abolitionists, proponents of the antislavery movement, was growing in the North. But not all slavery critics were Northerners. Some, such as South Carolina's Sarah and Angelina Grimké, came from slave-owning families.

The invention of the cotton gin in 1792 increased the production of cotton, therefore increasing the need for slaves to work the plantations.

THE GRIMKÉ SISTERS

Although they were born into a prominent Charleston family, Sarah and Angelina Grimké fought passionately against slavery. After moving to Philadelphia in the 1820s, they started publishing articles and giving speeches denouncing the practice. Because of their activities, they were threatened with imprisonment if they ever returned to Charleston. They never saw their birthplace again. In her article, "An Appeal to the Christian Women of the South," Angelina Grimké encouraged women to take up the abolitionists' cause:

I know you do not make the laws, but I also know that you are the wives and mothers, the sisters and daughters of those who do; and if you really suppose you can do nothing to overthrow slavery, you are greatly mistaken. First, you can read on this subject. Second, you can pray over this subject. Third, you can speak on this subject. Fourth, you can act on this subject.

Speak to your relatives, friends, acquaintances, be not afraid to let your sentiments be known. . . . Try to persuade your husband, father, brothers, and sons that slavery is a crime against God and man.

CRISIS AND WAR

South Carolina first threatened to secede, or withdraw, from the Union years before the Civil War began. In the late 1820s many South Carolinians were grumbling over the increased tariffs (taxes) on imports. The new tariffs bolstered Northern industries, but many Southern plantation owners feared that the tariffs would discourage international trade, making it more difficult for them to sell their cotton abroad.

John C. Calhoun was a Southern plantation owner who was in favor of slavery.

Vice President John C. Calhoun, a South Carolinian vehemently opposed to the tariffs, wrote a resolution claiming that a state could declare null and void any act of Congress it considered unconstitutional. President Andrew Jackson, also a South Carolinian, fought Calhoun on this issue. In 1832 South Carolina declared the tariffs unconstitutional and threatened to secede. A compromise was reached just before Jackson sent federal troops to the state.

As the years passed, debates flared in the U.S. Congress over extending slavery into new western territories. Most Southerners were afraid any restrictions on the practice might eventually mean an end to the slavery system and their way of life. In 1850 most Southern states agreed to a compromise that would allow slavery in only a few new territories. South Carolina was the exception. *The Winyah Observer*, a Georgetown newspaper, voiced a common opinion of the day, calling the Union "an engine of oppression."

The Republican Party was the party of the abolitionists, though Abraham Lincoln, their presidential candidate, held more moderate views. Lincoln was, however, opposed to slavery and proposed limiting the practice. On December 20, 1860, shortly after Lincoln was elected president, South Carolina, concerned about Lincoln's views, seceded from the Union, the first state to do so. Within a year ten more slaveholding states joined South Carolina and formed the Confederate States of America. In response Lincoln vowed to preserve the Union by whatever means necessary.

On April 12, 1861, under the orders of Confederate general Pierre Gustave Toutant Beauregard, cannons were fired on Fort Sumter. Though Fort Sumter stood at the mouth of Charleston Harbor, it was under the control of federal troops. As the shells exploded on the fort, Charleston on-lookers cheered from their rooftops, glad to be rid of the Union forces, or so they thought. Though the Confederates won the battle that would mark the beginning of the Civil War, the tide soon would turn.

In November 1861 Union forces attacked the South Carolina coast, capturing

The bombardment of Fort Sumter was the opening engagement of the American Civil War.

Port Royal and Hilton Head. Charleston suffered through battles, blockades, and food shortages, but the city did not surrender. As the war dragged on, the situation grew bleaker for the Palmetto State. General William Tecumseh Sherman and his Union troops created a path of destruction across Georgia and then turned north and marched through South Carolina to its capital, Columbia. In February 1865 Sherman's troops set the capital city ablaze. That same month Union troops regained control of Fort Sumter. The South surrendered on April 20, 1865, marking the end of Civil War, but not the end of South Carolina's troubles.

RECONSTRUCTION

At the war's end South Carolina was devastated. Its cities were in shambles; its countryside was destroyed. Although the slaves had been freed, most had no way to make a living. "The freed slaves were promised forty acres and a mule," says Alphonso Brown, a black historian. "Some got twenty acres and a mule. Some got twenty acres and no mule. Some got a mule and no acres. Most got nothing. Life was hard for everybody."

During Reconstruction, the period right after the Civil War, Northerners tried to control the governments of the states that had seceded. In 1867 Southern blacks began registering to vote under the protection of federal troops. The following year South Carolina was readmitted to the Union. A new state constitution was written and adopted by transplanted Northerners known as carpetbaggers.

In response to their changing society, some white South Carolinians joined the Ku Klux Klan, a secret racist organization. The Klan used terrorist tactics against African Americans and carpetbaggers. In 1871

By the end of the Civil War, much of South Carolina lay in ruins. Prosperous plantations and small towns were destroyed.

Klan violence escalated to the point that President Ulysses S. Grant dispatched federal troops to nine Piedmont counties.

Eventually, white South Carolinians regained power and set about reversing the progress African Americans had made toward equality since the war. A leader in this movement was Ben Tillman, who was elected governor in 1890 and U.S. senator in 1894. He helped enact laws that made it more difficult for blacks to vote. Tillman supported the growth of segregation, the legalized separation of blacks and whites. Signs for "whites only" and "coloreds only" were tacked up on drinking fountains, in waiting rooms, and at lunch counters, as the gulf between South Carolina's white and black populations widened.

DEBT AND POVERTY

There were other problems, too. Agriculture changed drastically after the Civil War. In just thirty years the average plantation shrank from 347 acres (140 ha) to only 90 acres (36 ha). "Although a few of the more prosperous cotton planters attained moderate wealth," writes historian Louis Wright, "most were lucky if they could boast a servant or two and keep their debts paid." The majority of the state's farmers didn't own any land. Instead they worked land owned by others and paid the owners a portion of their harvest in a system known as share-cropping. The landlord's profit was taken off the top of a sharecropper's yield, often leaving the sharecropper with little food on which to survive and with a large debt.

Life was not much better for textile workers. Most were paid wages that left them near poverty. Their children could not go to school because they had to work to help the family earn money. Some mill owners tried to create better conditions for their workers. In the 1840s William Gregg set up a village named Graniteville, which included homes for three hundred cotton mill workers, a school, and a church. Gregg's employees had the benefit of both a job and a community in which to live. But few cotton factories followed Gregg's example. Like sharecroppers, textile workers were stuck in poverty.

In 1921 the state's agricultural industry took another hit when an insect called the boll weevil destroyed half the cotton crop. There was an upside to this devastation, though. After the boll weevil infestation, farmers turned to new crops, like wheat and tobacco, which saved the state's agricultural economy. At about the same time many black South Carolinians who were unable to find jobs left the state to work in Northern factories, where they hoped to create a better life.

Children were forced to work in the cotton mills to help support their families.

WINNSBORO COTTON MILL BLUES

Thousands of textile workers who were lured down from the Carolina hills to mill towns like Winnsboro by the promise of good wages in the 1920s received a rude awakening. Men often worked seventy-hour weeks for an average take-home pay of eleven dollars. Women made only half that. Attempts to unionize were met with violence and bloodshed. This humorous song was based on the melody of a popular song written in 1919, "The Alcoholic Blues."

Old man Sar - gent sit - tin' at the desk, The damned old fool won't give us no rest.— He'd take the nick-els off a dead man's eyes To buy a Co - ca Co - la and an Es - ki - mo Pie.— I got the blues, I got the blues, I got the Winns - b'ro cot - ton mill blues.— Lord - y, Lord - y, spool - in's hard.— You know and I know, I don't have to tell, You

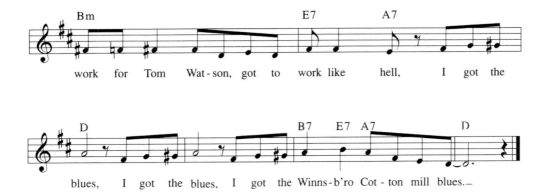

work for Tom Wat-son, got to work like hell, I got the

blues, I got the blues, I got the Winns-b'ro Cot-ton mill blues.—

When I die, don't bury me at all,

Just hang me up on the spool room wall.

Place a knotter in my right hand,

So I can keep spoolin' in the promised land. *Chorus*

When I die, don't bury me deep,

Bury me down Six Hundred Street.

Place a bobbin in each hand,

So I can doff* in the promised land. *Chorus*

*strip fibers from a textile machine

In the early part of the twentieth century many South Carolinians found themselves living in dismal housing. Many had not been given the opportunity to learn to read or write. Such diseases as smallpox, typhoid, and malaria ran rampant. South Carolina native Sam Kirby remembered his grandmother telling him that when she was growing up, four out of five schoolchildren had malaria. "My grandmother was the only one of the kids in her family who didn't have it," said Kirby. During the 1920s and 1930s measures were taken to control the mosquito population in the surrounding swamps, as mosquitoes carry many diseases.

POPULATION GROWTH: 1800–2000

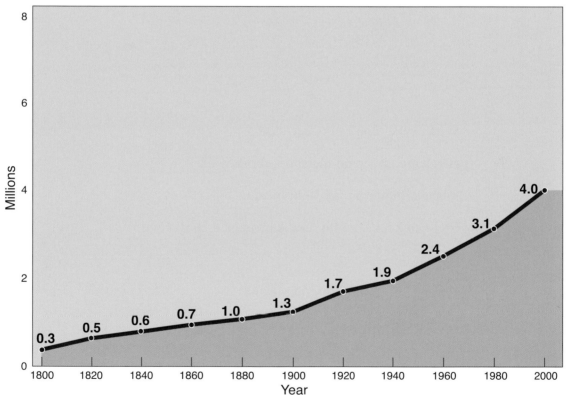

In the 1930s South Carolina's struggling economy took an even worse turn. Like the rest of the country, the Palmetto State fell victim to the Great Depression. Factories closed, leaving already poor textile workers with no means of support. Farmers suffered, too, as the price of cotton hit rock bottom.

It took a long time, but slowly life improved in South Carolina. Vaccinations helped curb disease, funding for schools and medical facilities increased, and new roads and highways were built. President Franklin Roosevelt's New Deal legislation created job programs that put many people back to work and helped cotton farmers reclaim their land.

THE LONG ROAD TO INTEGRATION

Besides the economic issues there were also social disparities that needed to be resolved. "South Carolina is now the only state which conducts a primary election solely for whites. It is time for South Carolina to rejoin the Union," wrote J. Waites Waring, a federal judge from an established Charleston family. Beginning in 1845 Waring supported equal education for African Americans and equal pay for black and white teachers. In 1947 he bravely fought to allow blacks to vote in Democratic primary elections, from which they had previously been excluded.

Judge Waring suffered because of his rulings. His home was vandalized, and he was shunned by friends and relatives. "We live in darkest South Carolina," Waring said after anti–civil rights politicians tried to take his job away. Eventually Waring and his wife moved to New York.

Waring's decision to allow blacks to vote was a first step toward gaining equal rights for African Americans in South Carolina. The process took years, but eventually laws enforcing segregation were

In 1963 desegregation began in Charleston schools. By 1970 all of South Carolina's public school distrcts were integrated.

thrown out, and racial division lessened. Though there were some skirmishes and demonstrations, South Carolina's schools were integrated in the 1960s. There was one deadly confrontation in 1968 in the town of Orangeburg, when a group of black students protested the segregation of a bowling alley. Police were called in to break up the protest, twenty-seven students were wounded, and three young black men were killed. Despite this tragedy, desegregation was finally a success. Then in 1979 a bronze sculpture was erected in the Charleston City Council chambers honoring the man who first suggested that it was time for South Carolina to integrate. The sculpture was of none other than Judge J. Waites Waring.

CHANGING ECONOMY, CHANGING CONCERNS

South Carolina's economy changed following World War II. Tobacco and soybeans replaced cotton as major crops, while new industries, many of them coming from the North, moved in and took over as the leading provider of income. More dams were built on the state's major rivers to supply power to the new businesses. Nuclear plants were also established, which helped make the state a leader in supplying nuclear materials for the country.

As industries expanded in the state, South Carolinians became concerned about air and water pollution. Addressing the health of the environment while still encouraging businesses to come to the state was a real challenge. Environmental organizations, such as the South Carolina Environmental Law Project and the South Carolina Coastal Environmental League, were formed to help ensure that the needs of businesses and the health of the environment remained in balance. Citizens and local and state governments worked together to ensure the continuing health and beauty of the state.

Production factories in South Carolina produce enormous amounts of smoke, which contributes to air pollution.

THE NEW RAVENEL COOPER RIVER BRIDGE

Before the Arthur Ravenel Jr. Cooper River Bridge was constructed and opened on July 16, 2005, there were two older bridges that crossed the Cooper River, carrying car traffic from Charleston to Mount Pleasant. The two older bridges were, at one time, condemned as the most dangerous bridges in the United States.

The older of the two stood 150 feet (46 m) above the river and in its day was the largest bridge of its type in the world. It was as beautiful as it was scary. The bridge lanes were narrow, and the drive to the summit was harrowing. In 1948 the bridge was rammed by a barge and suffered major damages. By 1970 the weight of trucks traveling over it had to be limited because of the extensive metal deterioration the structure was suffering.

To alleviate some of the stress on the older bridge, the construction of the second bridge, a 2-mile (3-km) span, was begun in 1961. The bridges each carried one-way traffic.

Those bridges are now gone. The new bridge dominates the scene, with its diamond-shaped structural beams. The Ravenel Jr. Bridge is a cable-stayed bridge, which means it has several columns, or towers, from which stretch cables that support the deck, or roadway, of the bridge. There are eight lanes on this bridge, which has a span of 1,546 feet, making it one of the longest cable-stayed bridges in the Western Hemisphere.

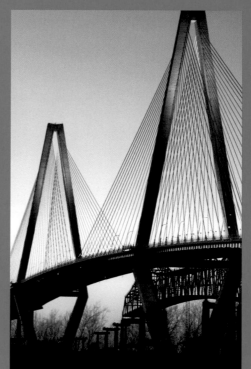

After struggling with social and economic challenges throughout the history of their state, South Carolinians have learned to welcome change. "In spite of our faults . . . South Carolina has astonished itself and others by its progress in our time. We have achieved a reasonable peace among ourselves," says historian Louis Wright. "From the mountains to the coast, [South Carolina] is a pleasant land in which the populace, white and black, can take pride and find satisfaction."

SOUTH CAROLINA AND THE CONFEDERATE FLAG

During the early 1960s, before the forced integration of schools and the passage of the Civil Rights Act, South Carolina legislators allowed the raising of the Confederate flag on top of the state capitol building. Some people defended this practice, stating that it was done to celebrate the hundredth anniversary of the Civil War. Others found the act to be offensive—an attempt to discourage the fight for civil rights for blacks. Behind these two opposing views are the two disparate definitions of what the Confederate flag symbolizes.

On one hand some Southerners see the Confederate flag as a symbol of the brave soldiers who fought and lost their lives in the Civil War. For them the flag represents Southern history and culture. For others, however, the flag is a symbol of slavery and memories of discrimination, torture, and death. These opposing views are all but impossible to bridge. So a battle over the Confederate flag in South Carolina, particularly as it flies over the capitol building, has been raging for more than forty years.

The National Association for the Advancement of Colored People (NAACP) has protested the appearance of the Confederate flag on state lands in South Carolina since it first appeared on top of the capitol building. These efforts have gained national attention in the past decade. After many years of negotiations between the NAACP and South Carolina legislators, the NAACP called for a boycott on January 1, 2000. The organization asked tourists and those planning conventions in the state to refrain from traveling to South Carolina. The organization figured this would affect the state's economy, which it did, to some extent. The boycott also drew national attention to the issue.

On January 17, 2000, the NAACP also organized a large protest in Columbia on Dr. Martin Luther King's birthday. Before the protest began, Dr. King's son said, "This is the kind of thing we need to do. The flag is a terrible symbol that brings a lot of negative energy. And while we believe the flag has an appropriate place, it just does not belong on top of the capitol building because it is not a sign of unification."

Under pressure the South Carolina state senate finally passed a bill on April 12, 2000. Under this bill the Confederate flag would be taken down from the top of the capitol building and flown nearby, to the side of the building, next to a monument commemorating the deaths of Confederate soldiers.

The next month the state house of representatives passed a slightly altered version of the senate bill, and the governor, Jim Hodges, signed it into law on May 23. The flag was removed from the state capitol on July 1. But neither the controversy nor the NAACP boycott has ended. The NAACP wants the flag removed from state grounds altogether.

In 2000, during the heat of this controversy over the Confederate flag, there was a presidential election. As the Republican and Democratic

After much controversy, on July 1, 2000, the Confederate flag was removed from the South Carolina statehouse.

candidates toured the state in search of votes, each was asked for his views on the Confederate flag issue. The same question reappeared in 2004 and 2008. Some candidates claimed that it was a state issue, not a federal one, and therefore should be decided by the state legislature and its citizens.

The question before South Carolina is based on what the Confederate flag symbolizes. Is it a symbol of the Confederacy or does it celebrate slavery?

Chapter Three
Smiling Faces

South Carolinians have a long history of fighting with outsiders and even among themselves as the colony grew and finally became a state. But today South Carolinians are better known for their friendly and welcoming nature.

POPULATION IS GROWING AND CHANGING

Due to the number of slaves who had been brought into the state, South Carolina's population, until the early part of the twentieth century, was mostly black. But when racial tensions and discrimination were at their highest, many African Americans left the state looking for jobs in the North. Though blacks no longer outnumber whites, African Americans are still in the majority in many rural parts of the state. But overall, whites make up 68.5 percent of the population, and many of them can trace their ancestry back to the first settlers from Europe. African Americans constitute almost 29 percent of the population, with about 0.4 percent American Indian, 1.1 percent Asian, and 3.5 percent Hispanic. According to the U.S. Census Bureau's 2006 report, South Carolina is the tenth-fastest-growing state in the Union.

South Carolina is known for its warm hospitality, gracious living, vibrant history, and Southern charm.

African Americans remain in the majority in many parts of the state.

American Indians were once a majority, too, before European settlers began claiming their land. Over time, however, most Indian tribes were either forced to give up their property or were wiped out by European diseases. South Carolina still has an American Indian population, though it is now very small. Most belong to either the Catawba or Pee Dee tribes.

ETHNIC SOUTH CAROLINA

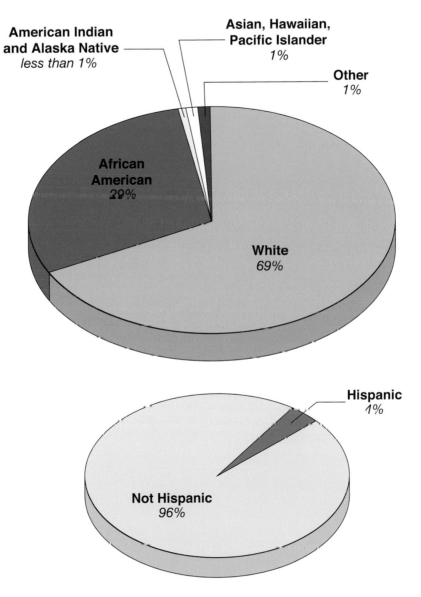

American Indian
and Alaska Native
less than 1%

Asian, Hawaiian,
Pacific Islander
1%

Other
1%

African
American
29%

White
69%

Hispanic
1%

Not Hispanic
96%

*Note: A person of Cuban, Mexican, Puerto Rican, South or Central American,
or other Spanish culture or origin, regardless of race, is defined as Hispanic.*

CATAWBA POTTERY

Evelyn George was ninety-three years old when she died, in 2007. For most of those years she made pottery. George was a member of the Catawba Indian tribe and lived on the Catawba Reservation, just outside of Rock Hill, South Carolina. The Catawba is one of the few American Indian tribes living east of the Mississippi that still makes pottery. It is a skill that has been passed down through the generations.

George gave demonstrations of her craft at the Catawba Cultural Center. She never used a potter's wheel. "I learned how to make pots when I was a little girl from my great-grandmother, my grandmother, and my mother," said George. "I get the clay from the same place my grandparents and great-grandparents got their clay—down by the Catawba River." Working the clay in her hands, she rolled it, patted it, molded it, and smoothed it with water. In about fifteen minutes she had made a seemingly perfect pot ready to be heated in an open fire—the traditional Catawba way. George made it look easy. Many times she explained the ancient art to visiting schoolchildren while she worked. "She was always an example for young people, that they could and should be doctors or computer programmers if they chose, but to remember where they came from, who they are, and what it means to be a Catawba," said Gilbert Blue, a Catawba chief, after learning of George's death.

While the majority of people living in the Palmetto State come from a long line of South Carolinians, the number of newcomers has been growing, especially since the 1950s. Many people have been drawn here by the state's economic opportunities, pleasant weather, and beautiful and varied landscape.

A great number of South Carolinians lived in rural areas longer than people in most other states. But today 60 percent of the population is clustered in the state's cities and suburbs. South Carolina's major cities are small in comparison to large cities in other states, but they are growing. Columbia is the state capital and the largest city in South Carolina, with a city population of about 120,000. Charleston, with its large military bases and shipping harbor, has a population of around 110,000, and its neighbor, North Charleston, has about 91,000 people. Rock Hill, the fourth-largest city, with a population of about 64,000 people, is located in the north-central part of the state, about 20 miles (32 km) south of the border with North Carolina. Mount Pleasant rounds out the list of five largest cities. The total population of the state was estimated in 2007 to be 4,407,709.

The capital of South Carolina, Columbia, draws people to the state with its broad, tree-lined streets and beautiful skyline.

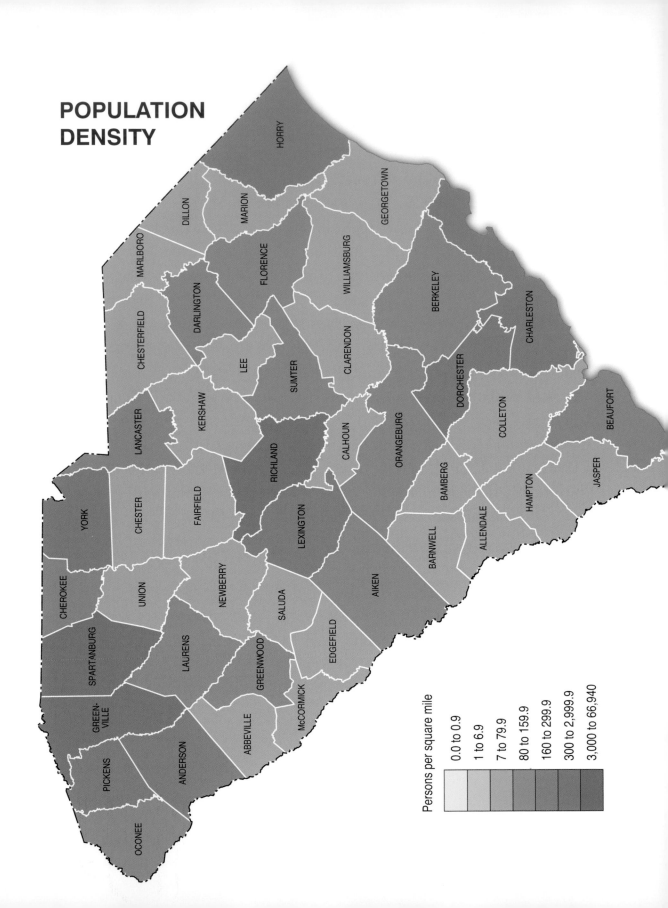

POPULATION
DENSITY

HORRY

DILLON

MARION

GEORGETOWN

MARLBORO

FLORENCE

WILLIAMSBURG

BERKELEY

CHESTERFIELD

DARLINGTON

CHARLESTON

LEE

SUMTER

CLARENDON

KERSHAW

DORCHESTER

LANCASTER

CALHOUN

ORANGEBURG

COLLETON

BEAUFORT

RICHLAND

BAMBERG

YORK

CHESTER

FAIRFIELD

LEXINGTON

JASPER

CHEROKEE

UNION

NEWBERRY

BARNWELL

ALLENDALE

HAMPTON

AIKEN

SPARTANBURG

LAURENS

SALUDA

GREEN-
VILLE

GREENWOOD

EDGEFIELD

PICKENS

ANDERSON

ABBEVILLE

McCORMICK

OCONEE

Persons per square mile

| 0.0 to 0.9 | 1 to 6.9 | 7 to 79.9 | 80 to 159.9 | 160 to 299.9 | 300 to 2,999.9 | 3,000 to 66,940 |

ROOTS IN AFRICA

The Gullah people are descendants of slaves, many of whom were brought to the colonies through Charleston Harbor. Many of these slaves were brought from western Africa and came with farming skills. At the time the lowlands and Coastal Plains of South Carolina were covered in rice fields. These were wet, swampy areas, where mosquitoes and the diseases they carried were prevalent. The African people were more immune to these diseases than were their white owners, so the slaves were often left for long periods of time on their own. The white landowners fled the area, especially in the summer, to avoid becoming infected. This absence of white overlords, plus the fact that many of the slaves in this area were from the same or nearby African regions, helped the Gullah people to maintain their own language and culture.

"I am a Sea Islander who for many years did not recognize that my religious practices, beliefs, and customs—so many things, in fact, that made up my very being—were African," said Janie Moore, a lifelong resident of Yonges Island and a member of the Gullah community.

The word "Gullah" probably comes from the Angolan language of western Africa. In South Carolina Gullah is both a language and a way of life that has been preserved by the descendants of slaves brought from West Africa to the islands off the South Carolina and Georgia coasts. Some Gullah are fishers and farmers. Many are skilled craftspeople who make baskets from island grasses, potters, or artists who create colorful designs on fabric.

Unfortunately, development is killing this rich culture. Condos, highways, and fast-food chains have displaced Gullah homes in many parts of the lowlands. But perhaps the most upsetting threat has come in the form

Basket making is among one of the many customs and traditions of the Gullah.

FROGMORE STEW

Frogmore stew is a traditional lowcountry concoction of shrimp, sausage, and vegetables. Have an adult help you with this recipe.

2 pounds Polish sausage, cut into 1-inch sections
1 large onion, quartered
2 quarts water
10 small red potatoes
10 small ears of corn
2 pounds fresh unpeeled shrimp
2 tablespoons Old Bay Seasoning
salt and pepper to taste

In a large pot, sauté the sausage and onion in a small amount of oil. Add the water and potatoes and bring to a boil. Add the corn, return to boiling, and cook for 10 minutes or until the potatoes are tender. Add the shrimp and seasonings and return to boiling. Cook for 2 minutes or until the shrimp turn pink. Serve with cocktail sauce.

of planned communities called plantations. These resorts have expensive homes, stables, country clubs, and golf courses. Their development has raised property taxes by 700 percent since 1990, making it difficult for middle- and low-income islanders to hold onto their land. To the Gullah community the new plantations can sometimes seem like an echo of the slave plantations of the past. "We have to put up with the 'reincarnation' of the plantation. It is not enough that the resorts are choking us out and forcing us off the island, but they're using a word that symbolizes so much hurt for us," said Yvonne Wilson, from Daufuskie Island.

Despite obstacles, many people born into the Gullah culture are working to pass on their traditions to future generations. "I know I can't save a whole culture," lamented painter Jonathan Green. "But as an artist I can help create greater awareness, perhaps. All of the change is not bad. But are they throwing out the baby with the bathwater?"

Programs run through the Penn Center, which was established to preserve Gullah culture, have helped native Sea Islanders keep their land and their way of life. "The linguists say Gullah is a dying language. Ain't nothing dyin' about Gullah," said Alphonso Brown, a speaker of Gullah. "Just last night, I heard a woman say, 'Dat food cookin' smell s' good mak' my jaw leak.'"

Each November on Saint Helena Island the Gullah culture is celebrated during Heritage Days. The three-day festival opens with the singing of spirituals and a shout, a religious custom in which people clap their hands and dance. Later, participants eat traditional Gullah dishes while enjoying storytelling, African dancing, basket-making demonstrations, and music ranging from contemporary gospel to old-time slave songs.

BRUH GATOR MEETS TROUBLE: A GULLAH FOLKTALE

In black slave tales small animals often tricked larger ones. In this story, told with some Gullah words, the rabbit symbolizes the clever slave, and the alligator the outwitted master.

Long ago all alligators has smooth white skin like they dressed up in Sunday suits. Bruh Gator float round thinkin' how good life in the river is. With all the fish he can eat he never have to work for a living.

Long come Bruh Rabbit, and Bruh Gator ask, "How you live on land?"

"Don't know, Bruh Gator," Bruh Rabbit say. "We see lot a trouble on land."

"What trouble is?" ask Bruh Gator. "I never meet up no trouble."

"Meet me in the broomsage field after the sun dries the dew up good and I show you trouble," says Bruh Rabbit.

Next morning time Bruh Gator find Bruh Rabbit sitting on top a stump, smokin' his pipe. Bruh Rabbit say, "You stay here, Bruh Gator and I go get trouble!"

He runs to the field's edge and puts his pipe fire to some broomsage. "Lookit that there yonder!" say Bruh Gator. "Ain't trouble pretty!"

Soon the fire hot gets close, smoke gets bad, and Bruh Gator take out for one side of the field. He meet fire. He turn around and meet it again. He shut his eyes, throw his head close ground, and bust through fire to the river.

Bruh Gator get out of water and what he find? His white skin is all burned black and crinkly up. His good Sunday suit gone forever.

"I've learned my lesson," say Bruh Gator. "Don't go looking for trouble, else you might find it."

PRESERVING THE PAST

"I like that old saying, 'Don't know where we are going 'til we know where we've been,'" said Ike Carpenter, a native of Trenton, South Carolina, and a well-known wood carver. Carpenter makes a habit of keeping family traditions alive. Like his father before him, Ike whittles peach pits into intricate designs, often depicting animals. He also carves spoons. With each handmade utensil comes a story about how it was used in the past.

Preserving the past is an ongoing activity for many South Carolinians. Charleston was the first U.S. city to preserve its historic buildings. And many of South Carolina's smaller communities have followed Charleston's example, gaining much for their efforts. Newberry, a small town in the middle of the Piedmont area, is experiencing a rebirth two hundred years after it was founded. The revitalization was sparked by the restoration of the town's 120-year-old opera house. "The town was dying and I couldn't let that happen," said James E. Wiseman Jr., a lifelong resident of Newberry who spearheaded the opera house project. After more than a year of work the opera house opened in 1998, holding its first performance since 1952. "The opera house is the catalyst," said Wiseman. "But we aren't just building a building, we are building a town."

CHARLESTON SOCIETY

Of course, Charleston is the ultimate example of a city preserving the past. And there are a lot of Charlestonians who take this matter very seriously. While displaying the best of manners and Southern gentility, there were once some Charlestonians who considered those who were not descended from pre–Civil War society as outsiders. "I realize there is still such a thing as 'society' in Boston or Philadelphia," journalist Charles Kuralt once reported. "But for sheer disdainful exclusion, Charleston Society wins all the blue ribbons." According to Kuralt, who wrote this many years ago, even rich newcomers could never be part of Charleston society.

There was irony in this story, though. Historic Charleston, where all the tourists flock to see the great Southern mansions that line the harbor, has some of the most expensive real estate in the world. Few old-time Charlestonians have the means to maintain these mansions. While it is not always apparent, most of the city's historic homes are now owned by wealthy transplanted Northerners.

But times and attitudes are changing. According to Marjabelle Young Stewart, a woman who taught etiquette to such presidents as Lyndon B. Johnson, Richard Nixon, and Ronald Reagan, Charleston was the most mannerly city in America in 1997.

Charleston has maintained that distinction, or has been in the top ten, ever since. Stewart said, according to a report from CNN, that Charleston deserves the title not just for the colorfully restored old buildings. "It isn't just Charleston. It's the people who make it so human and kind and loving." Other cities come and go from the list, Stewart said, but Charleston is always on it.

Charleston draws thousands of tourists to the city through other efforts, including the restoration of its historic districts and the strong promotion of its arts. Besides the art museums and outdoor stalls from which local crafts are sold, writers have often used Charleston and its society as backgrounds for their works. The classic opera *Porgy and Bess* was set in the city, as was the movie *The Notebook* (2004) and the television miniseries *North and South*, starring Patrick Swayze.

There are many historic mansions lining the streets of Charleston.

NEW FACE OF IMMIGRATION

South Carolina is not a stranger to immigration, but over the years the faces of the immigrants have changed. Since the 1990s the majority of immigrants have been Hispanic. Though there were Hispanic people living in South Carolina prior to then, this population has increased at a rate of 211.2 percent since the 1990s, making Hispanics the fastest-growing ethnic group in the state. South Carolina has the fourth-fastest-growing Hispanic population in the United States. For South Carolina the Hispanic population consists mostly of people from Mexico. Smaller percentages are from Puerto Rico, Cuba, the Dominican Republic, and countries in Central and South America. The majority of these immigrants are young men who typically work low-paying jobs in agriculture, construction, landscaping, and manufacturing. Though the Hispanic immigrants are settled in all parts of the state, most are found in or around the areas of Greenville, Beaufort, Richland, and Spartanburg. One of the reasons for this increased immigration is South Carolina's economic boom since the 1990s, which translates into available jobs.

Though the faces of South Carolinians are changing, the goals of the people of this great state remain the same: to live a healthy and bountiful life and to enjoy the beautiful surroundings.

Chapter Four

Governing the People

South Carolina, like all the other states in the Union, is governed by a constitution. A constitution is a document that sets forth the laws the states will be governed by. The constitution also stipulates the form of the state government. South Carolina has had seven constitutions. The first was ratified in 1776, when the colonies declared their independence from British rule. The current state constitution was adopted in 1895.

INSIDE GOVERNMENT

Like the federal system, South Carolina's government has three branches: executive, legislative, and judicial.

Executive

The governor, who heads the executive branch, is elected to a four-year term. The governor appoints important officials and signs bills to make them law. He or she may also veto (reject) proposed laws or parts of proposed laws. The legislature can override the governor's veto by a two-thirds vote. Other elected officials are the lieutenant governor, secretary of state, attorney general, adjutant general, treasurer, comptroller general,

The state capitol in Columbia houses the general assembly and the offices of the governor and lieutenant governor of South Carolina.

superintendent of education, and commissioner of agriculture. All are elected to four-year terms.

Legislative

The legislative branch makes new laws and changes old ones. South Carolina's state legislature is called the general assembly and consists of a 46-member senate and a 124-member house of representatives. Senators are elected for four years, representatives for two.

Judicial

Five justices sit on the supreme court, the state's highest court. They are elected for ten-year terms by the general assembly. The supreme court can hear new cases and those that have been appealed from lower courts.

Governor Mark Sanford's administration focuses on improving the lives of people in South Carolina.

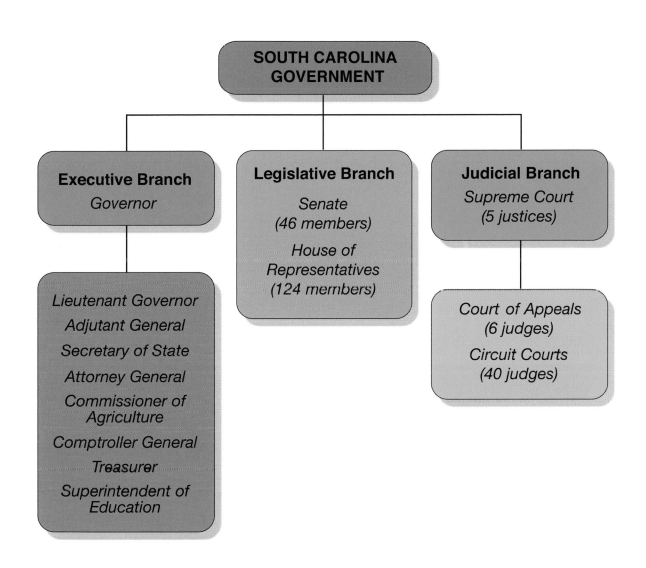

The court of appeals is the state's next highest court. It has six judges and hears cases appealed from lower courts. The most serious cases are tried in circuit courts.

Democrats once dominated South Carolina's politics at all levels. But beginning in the 1950s the Republican Party gained strength.

Until recently both of South Carolina's U.S. senators were longtime politicians. Republican Strom Thurmond was the first U.S. senator to hold office until he reached the age of 100. Thurmond died in 2003, just a few months before his 101st birthday. The other long-term South Carolina senator was Democrat Ernest (Fritz) Hollings, who served for forty-nine years. Hollings retired in 2005.

Replacing the long-term senators are Senator Lindsey O. Graham, who was elected to office in 2002, and Senator Jim DeMint, who comes from Greenville and was elected in 2004. Graham comes from Central, South Carolina. Both senators are Republicans.

Rising to political prominence, Strom Thurmond became the democratic governor of South Carolina in 1947. He holds the record for the greatest number of years served in the U.S. Senate.

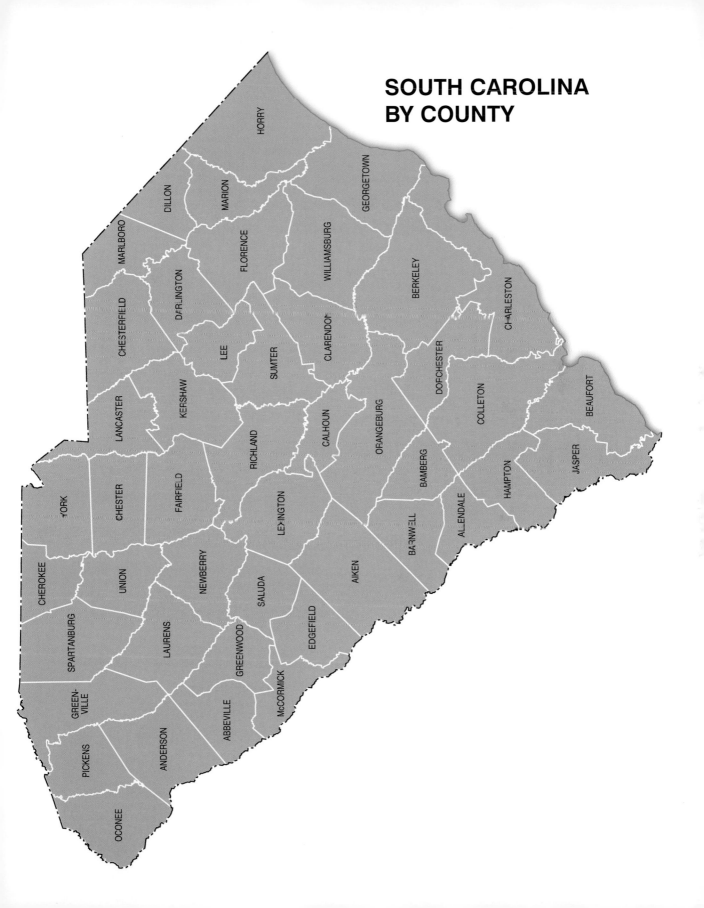

**SOUTH CAROLINA
BY COUNTY**

According to a June 2008 article in the Charleston newspaper *Post and Courier*, South Carolina schools rank among the worst in the country "by a number of measures," including the amount of money that is invested in the educational system. Many citizens agree and want to make changes. One of the first places some citizens want to start the transformation is in the state constitution.

There is a great debate going on in the state about the "educational standard" found in the constitution, which has been interpreted as meaning that the goal of the state government is to provide "minimally adequate" education for every citizen. Citizens would rather that the constitution be amended so it reads that the government will provide a "high quality education, allowing each student to reach his highest potential."

Politicians who are against this change to the constitution argue that the government would be forced into investing more money in the educational system, which means the state legislature would have to raise taxes. Many politicians believe that no one wants to see their taxes increased. Others argue that if this change is made in the constitutional language, citizens might then have the right to sue the government if it did not provide better schools. "Someone could sue the state and say it's not providing a high-quality education," said Glenn McConnell, a state senator from Charleston.

Those who are promoting the changes, such as Bud Ferillo, countered McConnell's view by stating, "If the state meets its responsibility for the higher standard [in education], lawsuits will not be necessary." Ferillo is attempting to gather a million citizen signatures to get an amendment passed. A bill addressing this issue would have to gain a two-thirds vote of approval in both the state senate and the house of representatives. Then it would be placed before the public for a vote in the 2010 general election.

South Carolinians are trying to make changes to the state constitution, which will force the government to provide a high-quality education to students.

Chapter Five

Wealth from the Land and Sea

Although agriculture once dominated South Carolina's economy, its relative importance declined sharply in the twentieth century. In 2006 there were only 24,600 farms in the state, and 78 percent of them had annual sales of under ten thousand dollars. Less than half of South Carolina's farmers listed farming as their main occupation. Still, farming is an important second income for many South Carolinians.

Cotton and rice were once the dominant crops grown in South Carolina, but today, even though cotton remains important, more soybeans and tobacco are grown in the Palmetto State, especially in the Southern part of the Coastal Plain. Peaches and corn are also major crops. Stands selling peaches line the highways of the upcountry a good part of the year. In Gaffney, a water tower shaped like a giant peach can be seen for miles around.

Tobacco has been an important crop in the state since the colonial days.

CELEBRATING THE EARTH'S BOUNTY

South Carolinians like to celebrate the bounty produced in their state. In June upcountry visitors can sample peach ice cream, hot peach cobbler, peach preserves, and pickled peaches at the Ridge Peach Festival.

The South Carolina Apple Festival in Westminster has been held every September since 1961. Fried apple pies are just some of the treats to taste. Many festival goers hang around to see the rodeo, complete with bull riding, team roping, steer wrestling, and bareback bronco riding.

Sweet potato pie is a Southern tradition, and some of the best can be savored at Darlington's Sweet Potato Festival each October. In April the small town of Lamar swells to more than 40,000 people for the Egg Scramble Jamboree, showcasing local culinary delights made with or without eggs, along with arts and crafts, a beauty pageant, and a dance. In October Bishopville hosts the Lee County Cotton Festival. This celebration features a parade, a street dance, a cotton picking contest, and the crowning of the South Carolina Queen of Cotton.

Chickens, eggs, cattle, hogs, and turkeys are also leading products in South Carolina. Chickens, hogs, and beef are mostly raised in the Piedmont and on the Coastal Plain.

The two-thirds of the state covered in forests supports a lumber industry. Softwood trees such as loblolly pines are used to make paper and paper products. Hardwoods such as oak, walnut, and maple are cut to make products such as furniture.

Fishing is another active industry in the state. Shrimp, crabs, oysters, and clams are caught off the coast. Inland lakes abound with trout, whiting, catfish, and bass. Fishing is also a growing part of the state's tourism industry. More than thirty million people visit South Carolina every year. Two-thirds of them head for coastal areas, such as Myrtle Beach, Charleston, and Hilton Head. Sea Islands such as Kiawah, Seabrook, and Fripp are also becoming popular.

Deep-water corals provide crucial habitat for commercially important fisheries, such as shrimp.

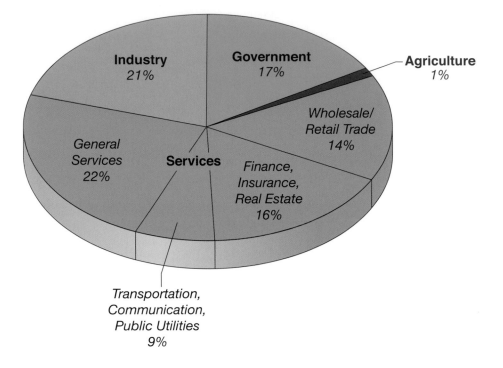

2007 GROSS STATE PRODUCT: $153 Million

- Industry 21%
- Government 17%
- Agriculture 1%
- Wholesale/Retail Trade 14%
- General Services 22%
- Services
- Finance, Insurance, Real Estate 16%
- Transportation, Communication, Public Utilities 9%

GROWING INDUSTRIES

South Carolina's economy was based on agriculture well into the twentieth century. When industrialization did come, it brought mostly low-wage manufacturing jobs to the state. Today the average South Carolina factory worker's pay is among the lowest in the United States.

The manufacturing of textiles such as sheets, clothes, and curtains is South Carolina's leading industry. But in the 1980s many textile workers' jobs were replaced by machines, and more recently some South Carolina textile companies have moved their plants to other countries, where labor is cheaper.

At the same time, however, many foreign companies have found South Carolina a good place to do business. Almost half of South Carolina's total investment in manufacturing is from foreign countries. Japanese, German, Swiss, and French companies have been building plants in the state since the 1970s. The upcountry cities of Spartanburg and Greenville are centers for international industry. State and local government and business leaders have worked hard to entice foreign companies to South Carolina. "The mood that has been set over time has created a welcome environment," said James Barrett, past head of the Spartanburg County Foundation. "One success seems to follow another." Today the state's largest manufacturer is Michelin North America, part of a French company that makes most of the world's tires. In 1992 the automobile manufacturer BMW built its first plant outside of Germany in Spartanburg County.

BMW's first plant in the United States was built in South Carolina.

EARNING A LIVING

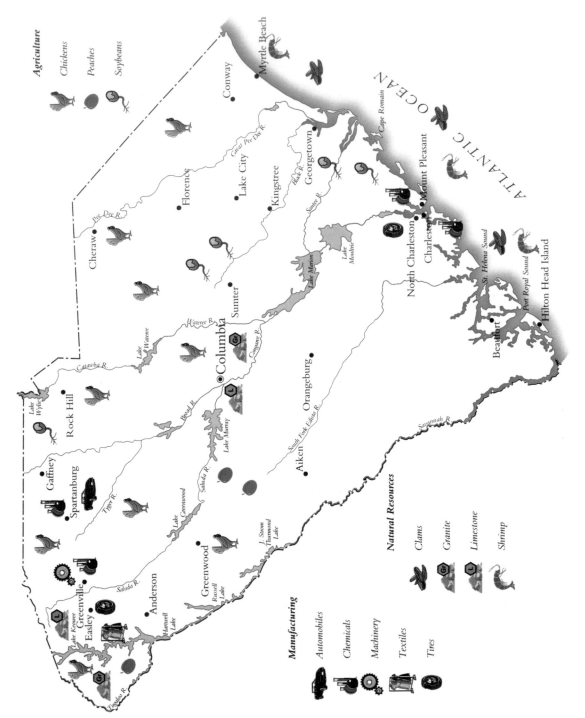

THE WORKFORCE

In June 2008 the number of people employed in South Carolina was 2,143,200. The unemployment rate in that same month was 6.2 percent, slightly higher than the national average of 5.5 percent. The majority of the population worked in the services, such as government, finance, tourism, and other business and personal services. The next largest group was employed in jobs related to transportation, trade, and utilities. The third largest group worked in manufacturing. In South Carolina the top manufacturing jobs are in the textiles and clothing industries, which in turn rely on the state's cotton crop. The state also produces chemicals, machinery, and automobiles.

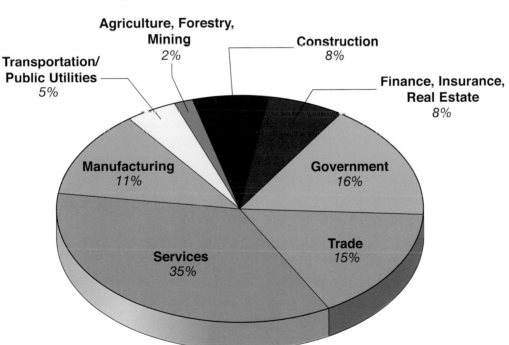

SOUTH CAROLINA WORKFORCE

Agriculture, Forestry, Mining 2%

Construction 8%

Transportation/ Public Utilities 5%

Finance, Insurance, Real Estate 8%

Manufacturing 11%

Government 16%

Trade 15%

Services 35%

TOURISM

Tourism is expanding in South Carolina. The traditional destinations in the state have usually included Charleston, Aiken, Myrtle Beach, Hilton Head, and Camden. People come for the beaches and the state and national parks, but they also visit the antebellum mansions and the well-established public gardens around the state. Theme parks, fishing, biking, and hiking are other things that attract tourists from all around the state as well as those traveling to South Carolina from other states. Tourism-related jobs accounted for 10.5 percent of the state's employment base, or about 198,900 nonfarm jobs in 2007. Tourism generates over $1 billion in state and local taxes.

Toursists visit Charleston for its rich history, tradition, and Southern culture.

THE MILITARY'S ECONOMIC INFLUENCE

Military bases in South Carolina have a positive effect on the state's economy. Local citizens find jobs on the bases, and military personnel buy products from local merchants. Military families often live off base, and visitors come and stay near the bases in order to see relatives who are stationed there.

There are several major military bases in South Carolina: Fort Jackson, Shaw Air Force Base, and McEntire Joint National Guard Station in the Midlands region; Charleston Air Force Base and the Naval Weapons Station in Charleston; and the Marine Corps Air Station, Marine Corps Recruit Depot, and the Naval Hospital in the Beaufort area. According to a study by the Moore School, a total of $7.3 billion in sales accrues annually to South Carolina businesses because of the military's overall presence in the state. Military facilities also support, both directly and indirectly, the creation of 142,000 jobs for the local populations.

Though the U.S. economy was struggling in 2008, people continued to flock to South Carolina because of the optimistic job outlook. With the state's favorable weather conditions and economic promise, South Carolina remains one of the best places to live in the United States.

Chapter Six

Beautiful Places

Hike up a mountain, kayak down a rushing river, fish in a swamp, or take a walk on the beach—you can do it all in South Carolina. History is well preserved in easygoing small towns and bustling cities. Celebrated gardens thrive throughout the state. "Smiling faces, beautiful places!" proclaim travel brochures, and they are right. South Carolinians not only love their beautiful state, they love to show it off to visitors.

THE UPCOUNTRY

The Blue Ridge Mountains rise from South Carolina's northwestern corner. The rugged beauty of this area is protected in the Andrew Pickens Ranger District of Sumter National Forest. Gradually the Blue Ridge's peaks descend into foothills, with fast-flowing rivers tumbling down the mountains. In all, the upcountry contains more than fifty waterfalls. Issaqueena Falls is among the most visited. Legend has it that an Indian maiden, Issaqueena, pretended to leap to her death to escape hostile pursuers, taking refuge on a ledge beneath the falling water. With water plunging nearly 700 feet (213 m), Whitewater Falls is the highest series of

Many who visit South Carolina enjoy taking a leisurely stroll along one of the beautiful boardwalks.

falls east of the Rockies. Raven Cliff Falls, a 420-foot-high (128-m-high) cascade, is one of the most breathtaking sights in South Carolina.

With all those beautiful waterfalls in the area, it is only natural that whitewater rafting is a popular sport in the upcountry. Chattooga National Wild and Scenic River draws many tourists and South Carolinians. It is the most famous whitewater paddling spot in the state. The river runs along the South Carolina/Georgia border and attracts boaters and hikers in equal numbers. The hills surrounding the area are thick with wildlife, and the river's Class IV and Class V rapids challenge even the most daring boater. The Chattooga River became a star after the movie *Deliverance* made its appearance on the screen in 1972.

For a taste of culture and history in the upcountry, there is no place better than Pendleton. Located in the northwestern corner of the state and founded in 1790, most of Pendleton in listed on the National Register of Historic Places. The town is the largest historic district in the United States. Pendleton preserves its mix of American Indian and African-American history and offers more than fifty buildings that were constructed before 1850.

GROWING CITIES

Some of the country's most rapid commercial growth is taking place near Spartanburg and Greenville, in the upcountry. Spartanburg has developed an international flavor by attracting many foreign businesses. Visitors may hear German, French, or Japanese spoken throughout this city. Historic preservation is responsible for one of Spartanburg's finest tourist sites: the Price House, a fully restored 1795 brick building that was once an inn for stagecoach travelers.

Farther east the city of Rock Hill hosts the weeklong Come-Sec-Me Festival every April. At this time many elegant old homes are opened to the public. Visitors can enjoy some peace and quiet at the city's Glencairn Garden, discovering acres of carefully tended daffodils, periwinkles, myrtles, and boxwoods, as well as a lily pond. Or they can cheer on the high-flying competition at the festival's frog-jumping contest.

TEN LARGEST CITIES

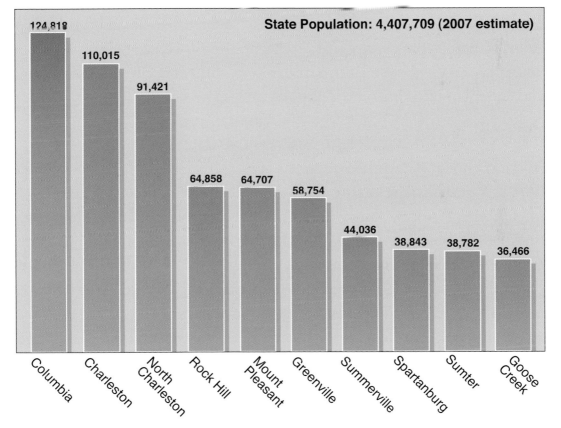

State Population: 4,407,709 (2007 estimate)

Columbia	124,818
Charleston	110,015
North Charleston	91,421
Rock Hill	64,858
Mount Pleasant	64,707
Greenville	58,754
Summerville	44,036
Spartanburg	38,843
Sumter	38,782
Goose Creek	36,466

SMALL TOWNS

Driving through the Piedmont is a bit like going back to an America long gone. Interspersed between woods and grassy hillsides are fruit stands boasting the best in South Carolina peaches and apples. Worn gray clapboard shacks—some advertising antiques for sale, others the best barbecue around—dot the roadsides, along with fireworks stands and signs advertising church retreats. Turn off the main road, and before long you are in the middle of a quaint small town.

"Chester County is the sweet distillation of rural South Carolina goodness—front porches, cotton fields, catfish and whippoorwills, dinner-on-the-grounds and friendly downtowns," said television producer Joanna Angel. Chester, the county seat, is charming and well preserved. Chester boasts a pre–Civil War courthouse, along with many historic churches and stately nineteenth-century homes.

CENTRAL SOUTH CAROLINA

Aiken is known the world over for its horses. In fact raising thoroughbred horses is such a part of life here that there are special stoplights just for horseback riders. The Thoroughbred Racing Hall of Fame occupies the carriage house at Aiken's Hopelands Gardens, which are known for their peaceful reflecting pools and curving paths. Next to riding, golf is probably the area's best-loved pastime. Aiken's Palmetto Golf Course, founded in 1892, is almost as old as golf in America.

Columbia, South Carolina's capital, is the state's largest city and its business, financial, transportation, and education center. Six bronze stars on the statehouse are a reminder that this city endured Sherman's invasion. They are placed on spots where cannonballs hit the building.

Columbia is home to many outstanding museums. The South Carolina State Museum chronicles the state's human and natural history. The Columbia Museum of Art displays outstanding European art. And the Riverbanks Zoo and Garden is one of the world's most innovative zoos, specializing in breeding endangered species, such as toucans and Bali mynahs.

The South Carolina State Museum, also known as the people's interactive museum, offers hands-on exhibits and programs in art, history, science, and technology.

Fast cars and festivals are a major part of life in the Pee Dee region, east of Columbia. The Darlington International Raceway is the "track too tough to tame." Twice a year it hosts overflowing crowds, in March for the TranSouth 400 and again on Labor Day weekend for the Southern 500. For more high-speed action visitors can check out the Darlington International Dragway.

Each fall snowy white cotton bolls cover mile after mile of Lee County farmland. Bishopville is home to the South Carolina Cotton Museum. Exhibits show how the fiber from the cotton boll ends up as the fabric clothes are made from. Visitors also learn about the history of cotton and see old and new cotton-picking machines.

The Southern 500 at Darlington Raceway draws huge crowds to the annual Spring NASCAR Sprint Cup race.

PLACES TO SEE

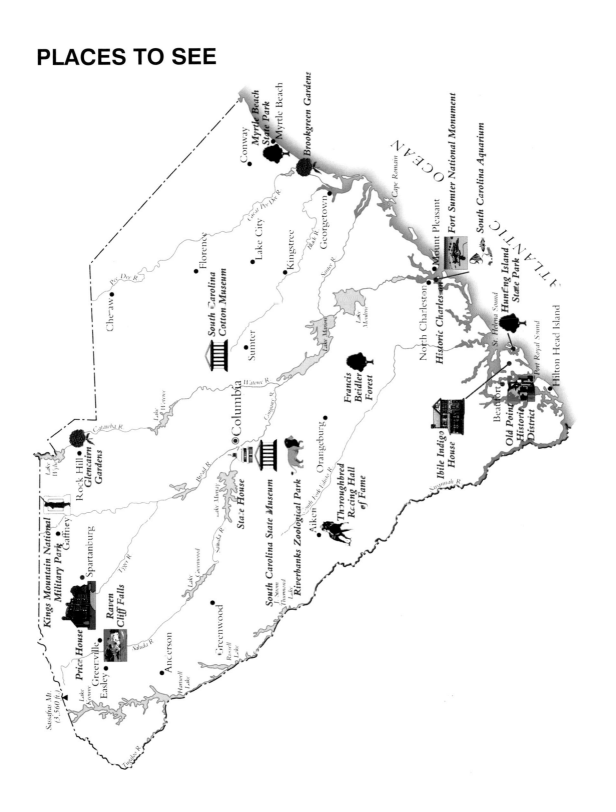

Myrtle Beach State Park
Myrtle Beach
Brookgreen Gardens
Conway

Cape Romain

OCEAN

Fort Sumter National Monument
South Carolina Aquarium

ATLANTIC

Florence
Lake City
Kingstree
Georgetown

Great Pee Dee R.
Pee Dee R.
Black R.
Santee R.

Mount Pleasant

Cheraw

South Carolina Cotton Museum

Sumter

Lake Marion
Lake Moultrie

North Charleston
Historic Charleston

St. Helena Sound
Hunting Island State Park

Waterec R.

Francis Beidler Forest

Columbia

Conaree R.

Beaufort
Port Royal Sound
Hilton Head Island

Catawba R.

Lake Wylie

Rock Hill
Glencairn Gardens

Broad R.

State House

South Carolina State Museum
Riverbanks Zoological Park

Orangeburg

Ibile Indigo House

Old Point Historic District

Kings Mountain National Military Park

Gaffney
Spartanburg

Raven Cliff Falls

Price House

Saluda R.

South Fork Edisto R.

Aiken

Thoroughbred Racing Hall of Fame

Savannah R.

Lake Murray

Saluda R.

Lake Greenwood

Greenwood

Lake Thurmond
J. Strom Thurmond Lake

Tyger R.

Russell Lake

Saluda R.

Greenville
Easley

Anderson

Hartwell Lake

Sassafras Mt. (3,560 ft.)

Lake Keowee

Tugaloo R.

THE SANTEE COOPER REGION

Swampland is abundant in the Santee Cooper region. The Francis Beidler Forest within Four Holes Swamp is the world's largest ancient cypress-tupelo swamp forest. Nearly 2,000 acres (809 ha) of trees tower over clear streams and pools, providing shelter for three hundred species of wildlife. As a wildlife sanctuary this forest is left totally alone—no attempt is made to lure wildlife to the boardwalk, no animal feeding takes place, no trees or flowers are planted, no fallen trees are removed. It is a swamp as nature intended it.

The Francis Beidler Forest provides shelter for hundreds of species of wildlife, such as this yellow-crowned night heron.

Lovely gardens bloom throughout Santee Cooper country. Some are planted on purpose, and some by accident. Such was the case with the Swan Lake Iris Gardens in Sumter. Hamilton Carr Bland, a Sumter businessman and avid gardener, wanted to landscape his home with exotic Japanese irises. Despite his best efforts, the flowers failed. Bland ordered his gardener to uproot the irises and dump them around a cypress swamp he had bought to develop as a fishing retreat. The following spring the discarded irises bloomed at the edge of the water.

At Cypress Gardens what were once profitable rice fields are now peaceful canals reflecting blooming azaleas, dogwoods, daffodils, and wisteria. Visitors can enjoy the lovely surroundings from footpaths or flat-bottom boats. Wildlife abounds in Cypress Gardens. Alligators, otters, and hundreds of kinds of birds can be found there.

Cypress Gardens is home to countless wildlife species, from tiny mosquito fish to the mighty alligators.

BEAUFORT AND THE SEA ISLANDS

At night the light of the moon highlights the marshes. Misty morning skies top islands of grass in shallow water. This is the lowcountry of Beaufort, Hilton Head, and the Sea Islands. The area's history is everywhere to see and touch—the history of Indians and European settlers, of slaves and planters, of war and Reconstruction and civil rights. Coming into Beaufort, it is as if the pace slows down to the clip-clop of horse-drawn carriages while visitors are given tours of the Old Point Historic District. The streets of historic Beaufort are narrow. State planners wanted to widen some of them, which would have required deep pruning of some ancient oaks' roots. "No thanks!" said Beaufort's citizens; they would rather live with narrow streets.

Indigo was once a major crop on Saint Helena. Today visitors to the Ibile Indigo House, an indigo processing studio, can see demonstrations of traditional indigo dyeing techniques from West Africa. They include tie-dyeing, using string to tie hundreds of small knots in fabric, and batiking, a method that uses wax to create designs on fabric.

A short drive from Beaufort is Hunting Island, the only barrier island reachable by car that remains essentially wild. A boardwalk through a forest of live oak, palmetto, and loblolly pine leads to a gorgeous beach. A climb to the top of the nineteenth-century lighthouse gives a view of the entire region.

Daufuskie, Edisto, and Fripp islands all have both resorts and unspoiled natural areas. Not connected to the mainland until 1956, Hilton Head Island boomed when a bridge was built. Today Hilton Head is one of the most popular resort areas in the East. Its wide white beaches are lined with luxury high-rise hotels and championship golf courses.

Hilton Head is known to many as one of the greatest golf vacation destinations.

CHARLESTON

"Charleston is the spiritual center of the South," wrote one Southern attorney. It is also often referred to as the Holy City because there seems to be a church on every corner. Whatever it is called, this city that survived war and Reconstruction, earthquakes and hurricanes, remains an elegant reminder of the Old South.

At least 850 buildings constructed before the Civil War still stand in Charleston, and most of them have been painstakingly restored. Horse-drawn carriages take visitors through the historic district, past homes such as one once owned by David Ramsay, a Revolutionary War hero and surgeon who introduced the smallpox vaccine to Charleston. They might see the house of Confederate brigadier general Pierre Gustave Toutant Beauregard—pirate treasure is rumored to be buried on its grounds. Down by the harbor is the DeSaussure House. From its wide porches Charlestonians cheered as the first shots of the Civil War burst over Fort Sumter. This and many other homes have enormously thick walls that have saved them from the ravages of time. Most have piazzas—large two- or three-story porches. Before air-conditioning, wealthy Charlestonians slept out on their piazzas in the summertime.

A great way to see Charleston is by taking a horse-drawn carriage ride around the city.

Charleston abounds with culture. In early summer the Spoleto Festival celebrates the city's fine arts. Operas are performed, new and old plays are produced, the Charleston Symphony Orchestra swells with music, and the Charleston Ballet Theatre puts on three performances a day.

THE SOUTH CAROLINA AQUARIUM

Charleston is proud of its newest attraction, the South Carolina Aquarium. This recent addition to the city blends into the natural and urban environment while showcasing the state's ecosystems. Projecting out 200 feet (61 m) over the Cooper River, the aquarium is a constant reminder of the relationship between the exhibits and the waters of the harbor, where dolphins, otters, and ospreys may be spied. The aquarium boasts many more animals than just those that live in the ocean. You can also see upcountry freshwater fish, such as catfish, bass, and bluegills; swamp-dwelling reptiles, such as alligators and snapping turtles; and residents of the Sea Islands, such as loggerhead turtles. Exhibits re-create the varied wetlands of the Palmetto State, from a mountain waterfall to a spongy swamp floor to a great ocean tank where hundreds of fish live with sharks and sea turtles.

Christopher Andrews, the aquarium's executive director, hopes it will encourage involvement in the "mystery, magic and spectacle" of South Carolina's environment. "Without a doubt, education is the link between awareness and action," says Andrews. "Our mission is to educate visitors on the many ways in which they can help protect our natural world."

THE GRAND STRAND

From Little River south to Pawleys Island, white sand and ocean surf dominate the landscape. With 60 miles (97 km) of wide beach, the Grand Strand is a popular summer vacation spot.

History buffs and island lovers should visit Murrells Inlet. There they can tour the Hermitage, an 1842 house that is said to be haunted. According to legend the ghost of a young woman named Alice returns frequently to a nearby marsh. Alice died after a tragic love affair, and it is said that late at night she searches for her lost engagement ring.

Pawleys Island, located on the South Carolina coast, is a large beach vacation community. The sandy barrier stretches 3 miles (5 km) long and about a quarter of a mile (0.4 km) wide.

Brookgreen Gardens, a unique 9,000 acre (3,642 ha) park, preserves the native flowering plants, and displays objects of art.

Not far from Murrells Inlet are South Carolina's unique Brookgreen Gardens. Scattered among beautifully tended shrubs and flowers are some five hundred sculptures. Included are works by some of America's most famous sculptors, such as Daniel Chester French and Frederic Remington.

Live shows and demonstrations are part of the educational experience at Barefoot Landing's Alligator Adventure. Albino American alligators, dwarf crocodiles, giant snakes, and other exotic wildlife can all be seen at this unusual research institute.

No matter where you go in South Carolina, people will be happy to help you find your way as you share in their state's beauty and rich history.

THE FLAG: *The state flag shows a white crescent moon and palmetto—the state tree—against a blue background. It was adopted in 1861.*

THE SEAL: *A palmetto tree rises above a dead oak tree on South Carolina's seal. The palmetto represents the fort made of palmetto logs that withstood bombardment by British ships made of oak during the Revolutionary War, saving Charleston. The seal was authorized in 1776.*

State Survey

Statehood: May 23, 1788

Origin of Name: Named after King Charles I of England. *Carolina* is Latin for "Charles."

Nickname: Palmetto State

Capital: Columbia

Motto: While I Breathe, I Hope

Bird: Carolina wren

Flower: Yellow jessamine

Tree: Palmetto

Fish: Striped bass

Animal: White-tailed deer

Gemstone: Amethyst

Stone: Blue granite

Carolina wren

Yellow jessamine

"CAROLINA"

Henry Timrod, who wrote the poem "Carolina," was known as the poet laureate of the Confederacy. The song was adopted as the official state song on February 11, 1911.

Words by Henry Timrod

Music by Anne Custis Burgess

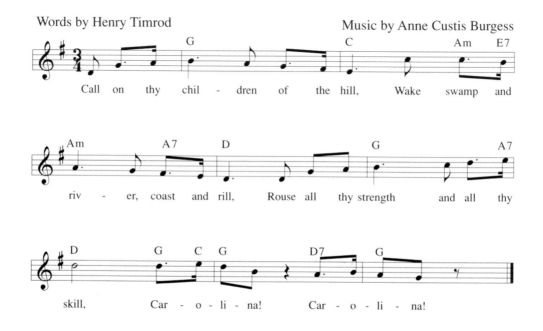

Call on thy chil - dren of the hill, Wake swamp and
riv - er, coast and rill, Rouse all thy strength and all thy
skill, Car - o - li - na! Car - o - li - na!

GEOGRAPHY

Highest Point: 3,560 feet (1,085 m) above sea level, at Sassafras Mountain

Lowest Point: sea level along the coast

Area: 32,020 square miles (82,931 sq km)

Greatest Distance, North to South: 219 miles (352 km)

Greatest Distance, East to West: 273 miles (439 km)

Bordering States: North Carolina to the north, Georgia to the west

Hottest Recorded Temperature: 111 ºF (44 ºC) in Blackville on September 4, 1925; in Calhoun Falls on September 8, 1925; and in Camden on June 28, 1954

Coldest Recorded Temperature: −19 ºF (−28 ºC) at Caesars Head on January 18, 1985

Average Annual Precipitation: 48 inches (122 cm)

Major Rivers: Ashley, Broad, Combahee, Cooper, Edisto, Pee Dee, Saluda, Santee, Savannah

Major Lakes: Greenwood, Hartwell, Joacassee, Keowee, Marion, Moultrie, Murray, Thurmond, Wateree, Wylie

Trees: beech, cottonwood, cypress, hemlock, hickory, magnolia, maple, oak, palmetto, pine, sweet gum

Wild Plants: azalea, honeysuckle, mountain laurel, rhododendron, Spanish moss, sweet bay, yucca

Animals: alligator, black bear, cottontail rabbit, dolphin, fox, fox squirrel, raccoon, shark, sperm whale, wildcat

Alligator

Birds: duck, egret, mourning dove, oriole oystercatcher, pelican, quail, swallow, thrush, wild turkey, willet

Fish: bass, bream, flounder, grunt, menhaden, rockfish, shad, sturgeon, trout

Endangered Animals: American peregrine falcon, Carolina heelsplitter, Indiana bat, red-cockaded woodpecker, West Indian manatee, wood stork

Endangered Plants: American chaffseed, black-spored quillwort, bunched arrowhead, Canby's dropwort, harperella, Michaux's sumac, mountain sweet pitcher-plant, persistent trillium, pondberry, relict trillium, rough-leaved loosestrife, Schweinitz's sunflower, smooth coneflower

Oriole oystercatcher

11,000 B.C.E. First people populate the area that is now South Carolina.

1400s The Catawba, Cherokee, Yamasee, and many other Indian tribes live in what is now South Carolina.

1521 Spaniard Francisco Gordillo leads an expedition along the Carolina coast.

1526 Spaniard Lucas Vásquez de Ayllón establishes San Miguel de Gualdape, the first European settlement in what would become the United States, near present-day Georgetown.

1670 English settlers establish South Carolina's first permanent European settlement at Albemarle Point.

1698 The American colonies' first government-supported lending library is established in Charles Town (renamed Charleston in 1783).

1712 North and South Carolina become separate colonies.

1717–1718 The pirate known as Blackbeard wreaks havoc on the Carolina coast.

1719 South Carolinians "revolt" against proprietary government.

1773 The first museum in the American colonies opens in Charles Town.

1775 The Revolutionary War begins.

1780 Colonists defeat the British at the Battle of Kings Mountain, a turning point in the war.

1788 South Carolina becomes the eighth state.

1790 Columbia becomes South Carolina's capital.

1822 Denmark Vesey tries to organize a slave rebellion.

1830 The nation's first steam locomotive to be placed in regular service begins operation in Charleston.

1832 South Carolina passes the Ordinance of Nullification.

1860 South Carolina becomes the first state to secede from the Union.

1861 The Civil War begins when Confederate troops fire on Fort Sumter in Charleston Harbor.

1865 Sherman's troops march from Savannah to Columbia. One-third of the capital is burned.

1866 Charleston earthquake kills eighty-three people and causes extensive damage to Charleston, Summerville, and Augusta.

1868 South Carolina is readmitted to the Union.

1893 More than a thousand people along the South Carolina coast die in a hurricane.

1895 South Carolina adopts its seventh and present constitution.

1921 Boll weevils destroy half of the state's cotton crop.

1922 For the first time in more than one hundred years, more whites than blacks live in South Carolina.

1941–1945 The United States participates in World War II.

1948 Governor Strom Thurmond runs for president as the Dixiecrat Party candidate.

1963 South Carolina begins integrating its public schools.

1974 James B. Edwards is the first Republican governor of South Carolina since 1874.

1989 Hurricane Hugo devastates South Carolina, causing $5 billion in damage.

2000 Pressure is applied from inside and outside the state for the state legislature to take down the Confederate flag from atop the state capitol.

2003 Strom Thurmond, the oldest U.S. senator to hold office, dies.

2003 President George W. Bush creates the Congaree National Park, South Carolina's first national park.

2005 The Arthur Ravenel Jr. Bridge, which crosses the Cooper River, is opened; it is the largest cable-stayed bridge in the Western Hemisphere.

2008 South Carolina is listed as the second best state in which to do business in terms of its workforce.

ECONOMY

Agricultural Products: beef cattle, chickens, corn, cotton, eggs, greenhouse and nursery products, hogs, soybeans, tobacco

Manufactured Products: chemicals, electrical equipment, machinery, paper products, textiles, tires

Natural Resources: clams, granite, kaolin, limestone, sand and gravel, shrimp, timber

Business and Trade: banking, real estate, tourism, wholesale and retail trade

Cotton

Battle of Cowpens Each January history buffs gather at the battlefield near Gaffney to watch reenactments of this Revolutionary War battle.

Triple Crown Aiken shows off its horse heritage each March with three weekends of racing.

Festival of Houses and Gardens Visitors can explore Charleston's extraordinary architecture and gardens during March and April, when more than one hundred historic homes and gardens are open for touring.

Springfield Frog Jump Young and old alike enter their favorite frogs in this April event to see which can cover the greatest distance in three jumps. The winner goes to the National Jump-Off in California.

Colleton County Rice Festival Rice-cooking contests and a soapbox derby are part of the fun at this April event in Walterboro, but some people come just to see the world's largest pot of rice.

Triple Crown

Spoleto Festival USA In late May and early June Charleston hosts one of the world's premier arts festivals, which features opera, dance, jazz, classical music, theater, visual arts, and much more.

Spoleto Festival USA

Gullah Festival The arts, language, and culture of the Gullah people are honored at this May festival in Beaufort.

Freedom Weekend Aloft Each May the skies around Anderson are filled with colorful hot-air balloons.

South Carolina Peach Festival Gaffney is so proud of its role as a peach-growing center that its water tower is shaped like a peach. Each July the town celebrates its peachy history with a festival featuring cobblers, pies, and slushes, along with parades, music, and fireworks.

Pageland Watermelon Festival This July festival in Pageland features standard watermelon-related events, such as seed-spitting contests. But it is also proud of its more unusual competitions, such as a relay race in which the runners must carry 25-pound watermelons and a race in which contestants riding lawn mowers must stop to eat watermelon slices.

Okra Strut Each September tens of thousands of people travel to Irmo to honor that much-maligned vegetable, okra. There are okra-eating and okra-cooking competitions and contests for the longest okra. You might even see people dressed as okra wandering the grounds.

Chitlin Strut Each November the population of Salley balloons from 500 to 50,000. People come from far and wide to devour several tons of chitlins, the fried small intestines of pigs. They might also enjoy a dance competition and a hog-calling contest.

Candlelight Tour of Homes Some of Camden's most beautiful historic buildings are decked out in holiday finery for the Christmas season.

STATE STARS

Mary McLeod Bethune (1875–1955) was an important proponent of improving education for African Americans. In 1904 she founded a school for African-American girls in Florida, which eventually became Bethune-Cookman College. Bethune also served as an advisor on minority affairs to President Franklin Roosevelt. In 1936 she became director of the Division of Negro Affairs of the National Youth Administration, making her the first black woman to run a federal agency. Bethune was born in Mayesville.

James Brown (1933–2006), from Barnwell, was considered the "godfather of soul" and was an extraordinary influence on popular music, with his hard-hitting rhythm and blues vocals. Brown began his career in the 1950s and continued through the 1980s not only as an entertainer but as a bandleader and a music producer. Musicians from reggae to hip-hop credit Brown for inspiring them. In 1986 Brown became one of the first inductees into the Rock and Roll Hall of Fame.

James Brown

John C. Calhoun (1782–1850) was a leading defender of states' rights and slavery. During his long career he served as a U.S. representative, a U.S. senator, secretary of war, and secretary of state. While serving as vice president, from 1825 to 1832, Calhoun argued that a state could declare federal laws null and void. This led to the nullification crisis, when President Andrew Jackson almost sent federal troops into South Carolina after the state nullified a federal tariff law. Calhoun was born in Abbeville.

Alice Childress (1920–1994), a novelist and playwright from Charleston, wrote hard-hitting works about racism and other social ills. Childress began her career as an actor and theater director before turning her attention to writing plays. In 1952 Childress became the first black woman ever to have a play produced in America, when *Gold Through the Trees* was staged in New York. In 1955 her play *Trouble in Mind*, about racism in the theater, won an Obie Award as the year's best off-Broadway play. Childress also wrote forthright books for kids, such as *A Hero Ain't Nothin' but a Sandwich*, about a thirteen-year-old drug addict.

Pat Conroy (1945–   ) is a popular writer famous for his entertaining novels set in South Carolina. Conroy's father was in the military, and his family moved frequently during his childhood before finally settling in Beaufort for his high school years. Conroy attended the Citadel, a military academy in Charleston, and then became a teacher. The year he spent teaching Gullah

Pat Conroy

children on Daufuskie Island became the subject of his novel *The Water Is Wide*. Conroy's other novels, such as *The Great Santini* and *The Prince of Tides*, also include elements from his own life.

Lawrence Doby (1923–2003), a native of Camden, became the first black player in baseball's American League when he joined the Cleveland Indians in 1947. A powerful, consistent hitter, he twice led the league in home runs and RBIs. In 1978 Doby became the second black manager in the major leagues when he took over the Chicago White Sox. He was elected to the National Baseball Hall of Fame in 1998.

Lawrence Doby

Marian Wright Edelman (1939–   ) is a leading advocate for children in the United States. Edelman, the first black woman to practice law in Mississippi, worked as a civil rights lawyer in the 1960s. In the early 1970s she focused her attention on children, founding the Children's Defense Fund (CDF). The CDF does research on anything to do with children and lobbies the government to see that all children get the best child care, health care, and education possible. Edelman was born in Bennettsville.

Marian Wright Edelman

Joe Frazier (1944–) was once the heavyweight boxing champion of the world. Frazier, who was born in Beaufort, was a relentless puncher, able to wear almost any opponent down. He won a gold medal at the 1964 Olympics and became world heavyweight champion in 1970. His win over boxing legend Muhammad Ali in 1971 is considered one of the greatest bouts in boxing history. Frazier retired from boxing in 1976.

Althea Gibson (1927–2003), the first African American to win either the U.S. tennis championship or Wimbledon, was born in Silver. Tall and strong, with a powerful serve-and-volley game, Gibson won both in 1957 and 1958. Gibson was a great all-around athlete. After she retired from tennis, she took up golf and joined the Ladies Professional Golf Association.

Dizzy Gillespie (1917–1993), a native of Cheraw, was one of the greatest jazz trumpeters of all time. Early in his career he played with leading big bands, including those headed by Cab Calloway and Earl Hines. During the 1940s he and saxophonist Charlie Parker invented bebop, a fast, complex style of jazz. Never before had the trumpet been played with such speed, drama, and surprise. Gillespie was a great showman, famous for his ballooned cheeks. He was also a talented composer, writing such classic songs as "Night in Tunisia" and "Salt Peanuts."

Angelina (1805–1879) and **Sarah Grimké** (1792–1873), the daughters of a prominent Charleston family, were abolitionists and women's rights supporters. After moving to Philadelphia, Pennsylvania, in the 1820s, they became active in the antislavery movement. They gave speeches across the Northeast, becoming among the first women to lecture publicly in the United States. In 1838 Sarah wrote one of the first essays by an American on the subject of women's equality.

Andrew Jackson (1767–1845) was the seventh president of the United States. During the Revolutionary War thirteen-year-old Jackson served as a messenger for colonial troops. Jackson became a military hero after defeating the British in the Battle of New Orleans during the War of 1812. Although Jackson was from a privileged background, after being elected president, he became known as a leader of the common people rather than the elite. He was born in Waxhaws.

Jesse Jackson (1941–   ), a Baptist minister and civil rights leader, was born in Greenville. While in college Jackson became an associate of the prominent civil rights leader Martin Luther King Jr. Jackson later founded such organizations as Operation PUSH, which promoted economic development for blacks, and the Rainbow Coalition, which encourages minorities to become involved in politics. Jackson, who twice ran for president, is famous for his rousing speeches.

"Shoeless Joe" Jackson (1888–1951), a native of Brandon Mills, was one of baseball's greatest hitters. Some people say that the great slugger Babe Ruth copied Jackson's swing. Although Jackson had many outstanding playing seasons, including helping the Chicago White Sox win the World Series in 1917, he is best remembered for being among the Chicago players who were paid by gamblers to purposely lose the 1919 World Series. Eight players, including Jackson, were banned from baseball for life. Many people prefer to remember Jackson's .356 lifetime batting average, the third highest in baseball history.

Jesse Jackson

Jasper Johns (1930–   ), a prominent painter and sculptor, helped originate pop art, a style that depicts everyday objects. Johns first became famous for paintings of flags, numbers, and targets. He later used three-dimensional elements in many of his paintings. Johns grew up in Allendale.

Lane Kirkland (1922–1999) was the president of the AFL-CIO, the nation's largest labor union, from 1979 to 1995. During his tenure he worked for equal rights for women and minorities within the union. He also tried to promote cooperation between labor and management. Kirkland was born in Camden.

Lane Kirkland

Andie MacDowell (1958–   ), an actress born in Gaffney, began her career as a model. When she performed in her first movie, *Greystoke: The Legend of Tarzan, Lord of the Apes*, in 1984, her Southern accent was so strong that another actress had to rerecord her lines. MacDowell had better luck later, turning in impressive performances in such films as *Groundhog Day* and *Four Weddings and a Funeral*.

Andie MacDowell

Francis Marion (1732?—1795), a Revolutionary War hero, was born in Winyah. After the British captured Charleston in 1780, most American troops left South Carolina. Marion stayed. He organized a small group of men who made daring raids on British soldiers and then retreated back into the swamps, where the British couldn't find them. From this he earned his nickname, the Swamp Fox. After the war Marion served in the South Carolina Senate.

Robert Mills (1781–1855), a Charleston native, was one of the country's first professional architects. He greatly influenced the look of Washington, D.C., designing more than fifty buildings there, including the Washington Monument, the U.S. Treasury Building, and the U.S. Post Office.

Jim Rice (1953–   ), a leading baseball player, was born in Anderson. Rice played for the Boston Red Sox from 1974 to 1989, helping them win two American League pennants. Rice was a strong, quiet player. In his heyday he was the league's premier power hitter. He led the American League in home runs three times, won the American League Most Valuable Player Award in 1978, and played in eight All-Star Games.

Robert Smalls (1839–1915), who had been born a slave in Beaufort, became a hero for the Union during the Civil War. Smalls had been forced into the Confederate army. In 1862 he took control of a Confederate ship and sailed it out of Charleston Harbor and into Union hands. He eventually became the highest-ranking black officer in the Union navy. After the war he served in the U.S. House of Representatives.

Strom Thurmond (1902–2003) was a U.S. senator from 1954 until his death, which made him the longest-serving senator in history. He was also the oldest person ever to serve in the Senate. Thurmond had a long history of supporting states' rights. In 1948, when he was a Democrat and the governor of South Carolina, the Democratic Party threw its support behind civil rights legislation. In protest Thurmond ran for president on the Dixiecrat ticket, winning four states. In 1964 Thurmond switched parties, which reinvigorated the Republican Party in South Carolina. Thurmond was born in Edgefield.

Charles Townes (1915–   ), a native of Greenville, won the 1964 Nobel Prize in Physics. While working at Bell Laboratories during World War II, Townes helped develop radar systems. In 1951 he produced the maser, a device that could amplify microwaves. This was an important step toward the development of the laser.

Charles Townes

Denmark Vesey (1767?–1822) planned the largest slave revolt in U.S. history. Vesey was born either in Africa or in the Caribbean. In 1783 his owner settled in Charleston. After buying his freedom in 1800, Vesey remained in Charleston, working as a carpenter. He eventually organized nine thousand African Americans, both free and enslaved, and planned to attack several South Carolina cities. But the plan was uncovered, and Vesey and thirty-four others were hanged.

Vanna White (1957–   ), the cohost of television's game show *Wheel of Fortune*, was born in North Myrtle Beach. White worked on the television show starting in 1982 and stayed until the show was retired in 2007. She also wrote a best-selling autobiography called *Vanna Speaks!*, published in 1987.

Vanna White

TOUR THE STATE

Fort Sumter National Monument (Charleston) You can visit the ruins of the fort where the Civil War began and learn all about its history in a nearby museum.

Patriots Point Naval and Maritime Museum (Charleston) Wander the narrow passageways of the submarine *Clagamore*, marvel at the massive aircraft carrier *Yorktown*, and check out more than twenty other ships and aircraft at this fun and fascinating museum.

Middleton Place

Middleton Place (Charleston) This former plantation includes the oldest landscaped garden in the United States, which was laid out in 1741. Besides the glorious flowers, you can see blacksmiths, potters, carpenters, and other artisans demonstrate their crafts and discuss life in earlier centuries.

South Carolina Aquarium (Charleston) Besides lots of fish, you'll also see turtles, alligators, and sharks at this vast aquarium.

Magnolia Gardens (Charleston) Famous for its lavish spring blooms, this garden contains hundreds of varieties of azaleas and camellias. It is also home to miniature horses and thousands of waterbirds.

Boone Hall (Charleston) Eighty-eight live oak trees line the entrance to this elegant plantation house, which was the inspiration for Tara, the estate in the novel and film *Gone with the Wind.*

Boone Hall

Myrtle Beach State Park (Myrtle Beach) Immaculate beaches, nature trails, and great fishing draw visitors to this park.

Brookgreen Gardens (Murrells Inlet) Giant oaks, pleasant gardens, and more than five hundred sculptures make this the perfect place to spend the afternoon.

Graniteville Mills (Graniteville) Get a feel for South Carolina's early cotton industry at this mill, built in the 1840s. You can also see houses, a church, and a school built for the millworkers.

Penn Center (Frogmore) Originally established as the first school to educate freed slaves in the South, today the Penn Center is a museum devoted to the Sea Islands' Gullah culture.

Penn Center

Hunting Island State Park (Hunting Island) Swimming, surfing, biking, hiking—this park offers endless activities. It even has the only lighthouse in South Carolina open to the public. Climb the 181 steps for a breath-taking view.

Gaffney Water Tower (Gaffney) This town has honored its peach-producing history by making its gigantic water tower look like a peach.

Hunting Island State Park

Kings Mountain National Military Park (Gaffney) In 1780 American troops defeated a far larger British force at this site, turning the tide of the Revolution in the South. After looking at exhibits and watching a film about the battle, you can tour the battlefield.

Congaree Swamp National Monument (Columbia) You can canoe, hike, camp, and fish in this unusual environment that teems with wildlife.

Kings Mountain National Military Park

South Carolina State Museum (Columbia) Feel the fossilized teeth of ancient mastodons, admire a car from 1904, and experiment with laser beams at this wide-ranging museum.

Riverbanks Zoo and Botanical Garden (Columbia) One of the nation's best zoos, Riverbanks is especially proud of its aquarium and reptile exhibits. And don't miss the sea lion feedings.

Francis Beidler Forest (Harleyville) A boardwalk takes visitors through the swamp that contains the world's largest remaining stand of ancient bald cypress and tupelo gum trees. Some are a thousand years old. A canoe trip through the mirrorlike water is even more magical.

Raven Cliff Falls (Greenville) Many people consider this 420-foot-high (128-m-high) cascade to be the state's most dazzling waterfall.

Raven Cliff Falls

FUN FACTS

The Charleston Museum, founded in 1773, was the first museum established in the American colonies.

Wood was so plentiful in South Carolina in the eighteenth century that only the "hearts of pine"—the centers of logs—were used to build houses. While this method was wasteful, the beams it produced are unusually durable. As a result many magnificent two-hundred-year-old mansions still stand in Charleston and other historic towns.

In 1825 Charleston native Joel Poinsett, the first U.S. ambassador to Mexico, returned to the United States with a bright red shrub. The plant, which in Mexico is called the fire leaf or the flame leaf, is now called the poinsettia in the United States. It has become the most popular plant grown and sold in the nation.

FIND OUT MORE

If you want to find out more about South Carolina, check your local library or bookstore for these titles.

GENERAL STATE BOOKS

Edgar, Walter, ed. *The South Carolina Encyclopedia.* Columbia: University of South Carolina Press, 2006.

Lander, Ernest McPherson Jr., and Archie Vernon Huff Jr. *South Carolina: An Illustrated History of the Palmetto State.* Sun Valley, CA: American Historical Press, 2007.

SPECIAL INTEREST BOOKS

Brooks, Benjamin, and Tim Cook. *The Waterfalls of South Carolina.* Columbia, SC: Palmetto Conservation Foundation, 2007.

Franklin, Paul M. *Backroads of South Carolina: Your Guide to South Carolina's Most Scenic Backroad Adventures.* Blaine, WA: Voyager Press, 2006.

———. *South Carolina's Plantations & Historic Homes.* St. Paul, MN: Voyager Press, 2006.

Marszalek, John F. *A Black Congressman in the Age of Jim Crow: South Carolina's George Washington Murray*. Gainesville: University Press of Florida, 2006.

Rhodes, Rick. *Charleston, South Carolina: A Photographic Portrait*. Rockport, MA: Twin Lights Publishers, 2008.

Zepke, Terrance. *Best Ghost Tales of South Carolina*. Sarasota, FL: Pineapple Press, 2004.

WEBSITES

Cooper River Bridge

www.cooperriverbridge.org

Learn about the construction of the unique Arthur Ravenel Jr. Bridge in Charleston Harbor and see photographs of it at this website.

Official Website of the State of South Carolina

www.sc.gov

At this website you will find information about the state government and history, and interesting facts and up-to-date news about what is happening in South Carolina.

South Carolina Aquarium

www.scaquarium.org/STR/default.html

News about rescues and releases of sea turtles are listed on the website of the South Carolina Aquarium.

South Carolina Information Highway

www.sciway.net

One of the biggest sites for information on South Carolina. It includes the history of cities and towns, current environmental issues, and a calendar of events taking place around the state.

South Carolina Official Tourism Site

www.discoversouthcarolina.com

This site provides information about some of the greatest places to visit in South Carolina.

Index

Page numbers in **boldface** are illustrations and charts.

ABOUT THE AUTHORS

Nancy Hoffman is a part-time journalist and full-time mother. She lives in Nashville, Tennessee, with her husband, Tony, and their daughters, Eva and Chloe. She and her nineteen-year-old daughter traveled throughout the state of South Carolina doing research for this book.

Joyce Hart has written and coauthored several books about the states. This book about South Carolina is one of her favorites, because she grew up in Charleston. Her father was stationed at Charleston Air Force Base, and she graduated from Bishop England High School. She lived on the Isle of Palms for one year before moving west of the Ashley. When she wasn't studying, she spent a lot of time at Foley Beach. Though she now lives in Seattle, she has fond memories of growing up in the South.